Dedicated to my Son. You made the choice to live. You perfected determination in your fight for life. We are so proud of you.

Remember- You know my number

~ Love Mom

Some names have been changed in this manuscript.

Order this book online at www.trafford.com/07-0993
or email orders@trafford.com

Most Trafford titles are also available at major online book retailers.

© Copyright 2007 Fern Norby.
Cover Design and Illustrations by Wanina Travis, Prairie Home Design.
All rights reserved. No part of this publication may be reproduced, stored in a retrieval system, or transmitted, in any form or by any means, electronic, mechanical, photocopying, recording, or otherwise, without the written prior permission of the author.

Note for Librarians: A cataloguing record for this book is available from Library and Archives Canada at www.collectionscanada.ca/amicus/index-e.html

Printed in Victoria, BC, Canada.

ISBN: 978-1-4251-2845-6

We at Trafford believe that it is the responsibility of us all, as both individuals and corporations, to make choices that are environmentally and socially sound. You, in turn, are supporting this responsible conduct each time you purchase a Trafford book, or make use of our publishing services. To find out how you are helping, please visit www.trafford.com/responsiblepublishing.html

Our mission is to efficiently provide the world's finest, most comprehensive book publishing service, enabling every author to experience success. To find out how to publish your book, your way, and have it available worldwide, visit us online at www.trafford.com/10510

 www.trafford.com

North America & international
toll-free: 1 888 232 4444 (USA & Canada)
phone: 250 383 6864 ♦ fax: 250 383 6804 ♦ email: info@trafford.com

The United Kingdom & Europe
phone: +44 (0)1865 722 113 ♦ local rate: 0845 230 9601
facsimile: +44 (0)1865 722 868 ♦ email: info.uk@trafford.com

10 9 8 7 6 5 4 3 2

*This is our story –
To God Be The Glory!
Jean*

Index

Chapter One — The Changing Day	1
Chapter Two — The First Few Days	10
Chapter Three — Searching For Help	17
Chapter Four — Making A Decision	24
Chapter Five — The Next Three Weeks	31
Chapter Six — The Journey Continues	53
Chapter Seven — What Would Today Bring?	65
Chapter Eight — Ongoing Care	83
Chapter Nine — The Gift of Life	90
Chapter Ten — The Perfect Match	99
Chapter Eleven — The Fifty-third Birthday	110

Preface

To Save My Son is a story about alcohol, my son, and his life saving donor. This is my story – written as a Mom. In this story I hope to describe with emotion, the struggle, the fears, and the hope that filled my life for a number of years. I am describing my son's fight to live. A fight that is waiting for anyone who wants to break free from the destruction of alcoholism.

My prayer is that others in similar situations will make the choice to reach out for help, before the day when a liver specialist looks them in the eye and tells them "You have one and a half years to live without a transplant. There is no hope for you without that procedure."

The thirty years of drinking was over, the next fifteen months were a nightmare. Each day brought a new experience and new knowledge that would save my son's life. In a way my son was very fortunate, (just as I was that he was my son). I was a healthy seventy-one year old woman, still able to drive in the city, and retired; thus I was able to put all of my efforts into saving my son.

Our home was the hard working home of a construction family. Alcohol was a part of that home, it was a work related social activity, and a way for the crew to relax, or so it was thought. I am not blaming the lifestyle that construction work brought to our home, but I take responsibility as a mother that I did not recognize the dangers that this would bring into our family.

As a child my son was always such a little man, he played hard, kept his room neat, attended Sunday school with his siblings and I, and did well in school. Then time went on an he joined the construction crew after his high school graduation. Construction is a physically demanding profession, which often requires long hours and hard work, sometimes after these long days, for some, a drink seemed to be in order. For Don alcohol became more than this.

Now I had the opportunity to help my son have a second chance at life, a good life. This is the story of my journey to save my son.

CHAPTER 1

The Changing Day

On the morning of August 20, 2004, I awoke from a troubled sleep with an ongoing prayer on my lips and in my broken heart. My eyes looked to the heavens as I prayed that my son had lived through another night. I quickly and carefully dressed, not knowing where, or what my day might bring. The motions came automatically as I tidied my hair, and added make-up to my tired eyes. The bed was made, I did not know how long I would be away. I hurried to get to Don's house as I did everyday.

As I put my hand on his doorknob fear rushed through my body once again. Would my beloved son still be alive? Many times each day I would find myself in the same place, with time standing still, praying, Dear God please let Don be okay. I slowly opened the door smelling an odour that lingered. The bedroom door was open so I glanced in as a I cautiously tip-toed by. Dirty blankets and clothes covered the room. My heart sank as I made my way a few steps further to the little kitchen cluttered with dirty dishes and unfinished pizza. The supper that I had brought the previous evening was untouched. I stood by the sink, hanging onto the cupboard giving myself a moment to find the strength to continue on. I heard my son call from the bedroom. His voice was husky and his speech slurred. I thanked God that he was alive.

"Mom," he said slowly, "go into the living room. I'll be right out. I want to talk to you."

As I sat on the edge of the couch with my fingers clenched, my mind was racing, as I thought about how I would deal with the next few moments. What would I say to Don to help him with whatever he had to tell me? Don came into the living room with his housecoat barely on. This was my son. The curse of alcohol had tightened around this fifty-two year old man. Each day for months I followed this same nightmare. I wanted to take him into my arms and make it all go away. However only Don could choose to make this problem go away.

He tugged at the soiled housecoat with shaking hands, his voice was weak as he said, "Mom I can't do this anymore. I am going to stop drinking."

I had heard these words before, but somehow I knew that this time it was different. His eyes were pleading for help. His once strong body trembled. This time his problem was much more than the skinned knees of childhood. It was alcoholism.

My fifty-two year old son, Don, had used alcohol as his friend, and a way to relax for thirty years. It had become his constant companion and way of life, it ruled his every day and night. I assured Don that I would be by his side to help him in any way that I could, while reminding him that the job of battling this was his to do. I would help – but he had to want to change his ways.

Swollen legs extended beneath his dingy bath robe, overshadowed by an enlarged and uncomfortable stomach. He teetered on the arm of the chair. I walked toward him and put my arms around him, he backed away because of his unkept appearance and state. Don knew I was in for the long haul with him. This man who was once so particular about his appearance had now become sloppy and untidy. His sweater would most often be worn inside out or backwards. Because of his swollen mid-section and legs, his jeans hung below his waist. Don's once brisk walk had turned into a shuffle. He wore tattered and dirty ten-dollar runners. My Son was in a sorry state. I felt sick and helpless when I looked at him. I longed for the well groomed little boy that I had once known. People would stop me on the street in our small town and comment to me on my son's appearance, and ask if I was embarrassed by it. I was saddened by it, but never embarrassed because I knew he was sick. I felt his appearance drew compassion rather than embarrassment.

I was sure he was ready to take on the battle with booze with my promise to support and help him. I knew this time was different because of Don's determination and his will to trust me, and to let me guide him down the road to sobriety and health. This was my son, no matter what he was like, he was still my son and I loved him unconditionally, and I wanted to help him.

I stayed with Don for some time that morning. I was

careful not to preach. I spent most of my time listening to his new, and changed plan for his life. He told me he was not willing to get help from anyone. He could break this demon on his own. He reasoned that others had done as much. In our own family, two of his uncles had overcome this disease without the assistance of treatment centers, or others. Don had spent three weeks at a treatment centre once. He had quit drinking for one month after he returned home. However, he soon began drinking again. His drivers license had been taken on three occasions during the past three years. Money was paid to lawyers for court costs related to his drinking and its consequences. He was hospitalized because of hemorrhaging and seizures. Yet, none of these previous events changed his drinking habits. Alcohol continued to be his constant and favorite companion.

Don looked down at his soiled housecoat and rubbed his trembling hands over his growth of beard. He slowly moved towards the bathroom to shower, saying "Wait here for me Mom."

As I sat on the couch my eyes moved slowly from the once spotless kitchen to the large table in the living room full of his plants. The once tall and straight leaves were hanging their heads in thirst, wondering where the loving care had gone, which they had known until this past year when the disease of alcoholism had tightened its grip around Don. I could see that they too were pleading for help, just as my son was. I went to the kitchen and filled the watering can with fresh cool water, this was a changing day for all of us. The greenery was longing for the care that it needed to thrive and flourish once again, and so was my son.

Don was ready to take on the task of filling his body with

only good things; to stop the destructive habits that were tearing him into useless little pieces. This was Don's rock bottom. It brought me sadness to see my son in this physical state, but it also brought me encouragement and excitement. I was thankful that my Son had lived to see this day.

After his shower we realized the next few days were going to be unbelievably difficult. The tremors would turn into involuntary movements, as his body did all it could to demand the alcohol required to sustain it in the lifestyle it had become accustomed to. His mind would have to be incredibly strong to deny this demand. I prepared to watch my son struggle with this new life he was choosing, I thought I knew the battle we would face. I recalled that the doctor on call in February (when Don was in the hospital) had prescribed some valium to help Don control the tremors that he was now experiencing. We got the bottle from the cabinet and the prescription read – 1 tablet every six hours. Even though I was well aware of the danger of valium and its addictive properties, I was also aware of the danger that alcohol posed in my son's life. I quickly justified the use of this drug, reasoning that valium was better for him at this tough time than alcohol.

Don was ready to go back to bed, he looked so very tired. The spider-veins in his face were broken and red, his hands were trembling. I thought, if only he could sleep. I hoped he could now that he had voiced his decision aloud. He made his way to the bedroom. I tidied his blankets and tucked them around him, as I did when he was small, once again praying for God to protect him and guide him through the coming days. I grabbed a bag and collected the laundry to tidy up the house in preparation for our new journey in life. We had decided that Don would take valium at eight o'clock that evening to give his body a little more time to free itself from alcohol. These decisions were made without professional help, they were based on the medical experiences of the past, and a mother's intuition. I moved toward the door reassuring Don that I would return soon. He needed to sleep.

When I walked into my own home I felt so many emotions. They bounced around my head like a ping-pong ball. I busied myself with Don's laundry and watching the clock. I kept asking myself – How long should I wait to go back and check on him? What should I take him to eat? Something with protein in it, I decided would be best. I was weak from exhaustion myself, and I knew the road ahead would be long and hard. I had a small lunch and a cup of my favorite herbal tea. Herbal tea and a homemade "healthy" cookie were my soothing blanket at this difficult time. Strength crept back into my body as I drank my tea, and I allowed a touch of excitement to lift me up. What a courageous son I had to make this choice.

Don knew his body could take no more punishment, every cell was starving for nourishment. His troubled mind screamed for peace.

I finished my tea and looked in my fridge for food to take to Don for lunch. Something that would go down easy, I thought. But like Mother Hubbard's Cupboard the fridge was bare. I panicked for a moment and then remembered that Don liked Subway mushroom soup. Soup and a small milk would make a great lunch for him. I quickly put the laundry in the dryer and hustled off to Subway – thankfully mushroom soup was on the menu that day. I was a familiar face at Subway as I often bought soup there for Don. The girls greeted me and asked if I wanted my order in a box. I wondered, did she see my hands shaking, and did she hear my heart pounding?

She passed me my order with a smiled, and said, "Have a nice day."

I felt of course she had no idea of the trauma that my body was in at that moment. Have a nice a day gave me the boost I needed – yes, this was a nice day indeed.

In five minutes I was at Don's door, balancing his lunch and my purse in my left hand, and reaching for the door with my right. My heart skipped a beat, it had been three hours, three long hours. When Don heard the door he called my name. I went into the kitchen to put the lunch on the table.

"I brought you some lunch." I called. There was no reply. I stepped into the bedroom as Don was struggling to get his swollen legs over the edge of the bed. Once again he wrapped his housecoat around himself, and made his way out to the living room to his favorite chair. I fussed with the soup and crackers as any mom would; for her little boy who had stayed home from school with the sniffles and a runny nose. If only we had those years back – what could I have done to prevent all of this heartache and pain? Those were questions I could never answer, nor could anyone else. I quietly prayed the Serenity prayer, this was the day I had to do what I could to stop this nightmarish merry-go-round, with the hands of God leading me.

Don finished his lunch as we talked about ordinary things, the colour was returning to his face. I sensed a feeling of relief and strong determination in my son. I recalled a conversation that I had many years ago with another person who had stopped drinking. I remarked to him that it must have been hard to quit. He replied quitting was easy, drinking was hard. I had long held onto these words of encouragement, and now was fully beginning to comprehend them. I started to tidy the kitchen.

Don said "Mom, I'll do that I need to keep busy." He seemed to get a small surge of strength, then told me he was going to get dressed and go out for a while.

I reluctantly picked up my purse, and some dishes that I had left behind from previous meals. My thoughts whirled in my head. What do I say as I leave? Surely words of encouragement would be appropriate, but what? Don was not one to get involved in long conversations, even short ones were limited. I quickly looked at my struggling son and told him I was proud of him.

"I'll be all right Mom, don't worry" was his reply.

My day continued in a reasonably normal way. I cooked a roast beef supper (a good protein meal) and at six o'clock set out with a hearty home cooked meal for my son. Don would never come to our home to eat, he had not had a meal at our home for years, alcohol always got in the way. For about five years I had taken supper to him each night, usually he was not home. Supper was left on the counter, not even in the fridge, as I was afraid he would not see it. I always wondered how I could change this pattern, nothing worked. I chose to continue my obligation as a mother to ensure that my child, now grown, always had food to eat. Was it the right thing to do? Some would say that I enabled my son to continue drinking. I did not intend this, I was only acting as my heart told me to – take care of my children. I was the only lifeline that my son had, and no way was I going to allow that to be taken away, no matter what anyone said.

I was happy to see my son at home when I arrived – for the first time in a long time. He had straightened up the tiny kitchen, been for a drive, and got a few groceries including a large bottle of Pepsi. While these actions may seem normal to most, to me they symbolized a new way of living.

The fact that Don's home was just five minutes from my own made my daily trips possible. At this time my life revolved around my son and the trap that he was in. By eight o'clock that evening, August 20, 2004, I made my way back to my son's. This was the time that Don and I had decided that he would take a valium. I felt comfortable with this and was thankful that we had some in the house. Don's hands were trembling as he took the pill. He was tired and we hoped this would help him relax and get some much needed rest. I offered to stay with Don that night. He strongly refused my offer. He knew that this was his battle, and only he could beat it. Alcohol had attacked his body from the inside out. He could no longer continue down this destructive road. We both knew it was time, but wondered if it was too late.

CHAPTER 2

The First Few Days

THE VALIUM was taken every six hours as per label instructions. Over the next few days progress was made as Don continued to settle into this new lifestyle. From the time that Don told me he was going to stop drinking I had never seen any sign that he had a desire to drink. This was significant in my mind because I knew full well that liquor remained in his house. Don had turned himself over to me to see him through this, as he knew I would not abandon him.

Don got dressed each day and did a few chores around his house. His legs were very swollen and I believed that the old shoes he was wearing should be in the garbage. His walk was still a shuffle, and he seemed very unstable on his feet. This seemed to be getting more uncontrollable rather than getting better, this confused me. Every moment of the day I was thinking ahead, planning how I would help my son restore his health. While driving one day I heard a commercial about the Good Feet Store. I turned up the radio and quickly jotted down the address. It was in a city only an hour away. It seemed to me the answer that my son needed – and finally an end to those awful shoes- new shoes and arch supports would help his unsteady walk. I was sure of it. I turned the car around and headed home to make an appointment at the store. Yes, I could get in early the next morning, the pleasant voice assured me. Things seemed to be falling into place. I was excited and sure that this would put an end to the stumbling walk. Don was willing to get up early and head for the city. His speech seemed slurred, and he was slightly confused, <u>but he was not drinking</u>. So I thought – How bad can this be?

We arrived at the shop and a young girl came to help us. Don did not understand the measuring of his feet, or why the imprint of his arch was required. I could see that the helpful young girl was disturbed by this. I went to the back of the shop and found an older lady and explained my circumstance and asked for her help, she assisted us with a great deal of patience, and we left with arch supports, and new sturdy running shoes. I felt that we had crossed a big hurdle – the walking was under control, or so I thought.

Valium continued to be part of our daily life – every six hours Don would take one. I continued to be very supportive of this as a mother, because my son was not drinking. This seemed like a much better alternative.

Each day that week I arrived at Don's home early in the morning. Sometimes I would find him still in bed, but he was always awake. We visited about regular things, the weather, news, what his Dad was doing, just regular things. I continued to be confused about why he was having so many problems walking, and the swelling of his body continued to perplex me. I thought these problems should be disappearing now that he was not drinking, but they were not. My mission was to get him to see our family doctor. This was the one request he adamantly declined. I kept checking with the druggist who knew about Don's situation and condition, he guided me as best he could, ultimately recommending that I get my son to see a doctor. I continued to ask myself, how was I going to make that happen?.

In the afternoons Don would work in his shop on small projects or go for a drive. He continued to waddle instead of walking as I expected him to. I had hoped that his new shoes, and healthy lifestyle would solve this problem. But nothing seemed to be working.

On about the tenth day of his sobriety I went to see him, but he was not home. My daily chores kept me busy for the afternoon. Suppertime came and went and Don was neither home nor answering his cell phone. I began to worry and wonder. My mind envisioned my beloved son on a country road with a bottle of liquor and I feared the worst. I was scared that all of the work and gains we had made together were lost. I drove from bar to bar in our small town. I was happy not to find Don there, but worried where else he might be. I went to the surrounding towns and checked the bars there too. My heart was pounding – not only was the fear of my son being hurt overwhelming, but I realized and came to grips with the fact that he should not be driving in the condition he was in. "Why had I not seen this before?" I questioned myself. I tried to console myself with the fact that at least he was not drinking, and this alone brought me much solace.

I had no idea how destructive alcoholism could be. I had read books on the subject, attended a few support meetings for the families of alcoholics, but nothing had prepared me for what the next year would bring.

I drove to the local hospital, surely his truck would be there I reasoned. But it was not. I entered the hospital, and as I approached the desk my legs were weak as I asked the nurses if they knew of any accidents. They said there had been nothing. I could feel their eyes following me out, along with their sympathy and thoughts, as they too were familiar with my story as Don had been in and out of the hospital. My next move was to go home and wait. After all, Don had always been pretty good at keeping in touch with me. The nagging question of why he had not called still haunted me. Once back in my kitchen I automatically set about preparing myself a cup of tea, a chance to take a step back for a moment and collect my thoughts and plan my next move. As I sipped my tea the stillness of the house was startled by a ring from the telephone. I jumped to my feet to see who it was. The caller ID displayed 'Regional Hospital'. My hand trembled as I picked up the phone.

"Is Fern there?" a gentle voice asked. "Fern we have your son Don here, he is okay."

I somehow found my voice and asked "Was there an accident?"

"No. He was brought in by ambulance. He was found slumped over the steering wheel of his truck at a stop sign." she said gently so as not to alarm me. I felt relieved.

Don had driven to the city to buy some special pieces of lumber for a project he was working on. Even though

Don could hardly walk he continued to build things to keep his hands and mind busy. His truck had stalled at an intersection and the effort to get it restarted had exhausted his already weak body, he slumped over the steering wheel from sheer exhaustion. Help came quickly as this happened in front of a fire hall, police and an ambulance arrived and Don was taken to the hospital. He showed all of the symptoms of being drunk. Once at the hospital they began to do blood work to identify what was happening with my son.

When my husband and I arrived at the hospital Don was drowsy and settled in for the night. I went to the desk to find out about the blood tests. I was relieved to find that there was no alcohol in his blood, rather an excessive amount of valium. Of course I was not surprised, but I also did not understand it. The prescription said every six hours, and that's precisely what we had done. It seemed odd to me.

The blood work that was taken gave the doctors information about how sick my son really was. His liver was very, very bad. The doctor sent his report to our family doctor with instructions for an immediate appointment. Don was resting comfortably at the hospital. His Dad and I returned home where I collapsed exhausted into my own bed. I slept soundly for the first time in months, knowing that my son was safe. Morning came early. I slipped on my housecoat and called the hospital.

"Yes, Don had a good night, and could come home after the doctor had made his morning rounds." The nurse told me.

During the course of the past couple of years there had been many little and big miracles, some of which we did not recognize at first. This incident was one of the interventions of God, which placed Don in front of a fire hall where there was immediate help, and no one was hurt in this incident. Don was in the hospital where he had refused to go. This was the beginning of Don's road to recovery.

Don was ready to come home when we arrived. The doctor explained that Don's liver could not process the valium, or any other medication, because his liver was only partially functioning. This explained the build up of valium in his system, thus explaining his unsteadiness walking, and moving about.

After this frightening incident, Don realized that this was bigger than both of us. He was anxious to get an appointment with our family doctor. Neither of us had any idea what the next year would bring. In retrospect it was probably better that we were just taking one day at a time. We were learning as we went, and what a lesson we had to learn. We now realized that Don was facing a health condition that could be fatal. This was confirmed at our visit to the family doctor. Don's legs were so swollen that he could hardly walk – even with the new shoes and arch supports! Don's belly was huge. We were frightened as we went to the doctors office.

Over the previous five or six years Don had been in the hospital for a few days a number of times. He would drink until he passed dry black blood through his bowels and vomited blood. On one occasion he vomited blood, enough to fill a gallon pail well over half full. The ambulance was called and he was rushed to the city hospital. He was suffering from seizures, vomiting, and terrific shakes. I stayed by his side, he was my son and I was not, under any circumstance going to walk away, even though I was often advised to do so. Co-abler was the word that had been used to describe me. To me I was a mother trying to save my son. Each moment of every day my foremost thoughts and prayers were for my son to beat this curse of alcohol that had consumed his life. Each time Don was in the hospital, the doctor told us that his life was in danger. Not even the trauma that he had been through was enough to break the hold that alcohol had on him. These previous experiences haunted me as we waited for our appointment.

Finding a reason to drink was easy, finding a reason to quit was not quite as inviting.

CHAPTER 3

Searching For Help

Our appointment with our family doctor was at eleven o' clock in the morning. We went inside the clinic and waited for Don's name to be called. I knew that we were not going to be in for good news. I was scared. I was hopeful that the doctor would be able to help us, that somehow there was some way to make everything better. As always my son's abdomen was huge, his legs were swollen with fluid, and each day he became larger. Don got settled in the chair at the clinic and I stood by his side. Soon the doctor, who had been our family doctor for over twenty years, came in. He held the report from the Regional Hospital in his hand. He told us that Don's liver was in very bad shape. He said he would book an ultrasound. That was the end of the visit. I felt unsatisfied and disappointed with the information we had been given, yet deep down I understood that the doctor was doing his job and that further tests would give us further information. We left the office without any knowledge of what lay ahead of us.

I got Don home and settled in his bed. This had been a big day for him, as moving around was an exhausting experience for him due to the fluid which had accumulated around his lungs. I came home knowing that I needed to get more information to understand what I was really dealing with. I contacted The Liver Foundation, they were very helpful and sent me a valuable package of resources in the mail the next morning. I think that they could sense our desperation and were there to help us learn, and give us the facts that we needed. This package would serve as a guide for our new journey. There seemed to be lots to learn, and it was all new to me.

On October 7, 2004, the ultrasound was booked, and we were thankful for it. In the time we spent waiting I began to learn a few things about liver disease. It was sometimes confusing, but created a picture and an understanding for both Don and I so we could understand what was happening in his extremely sick body.

Some of the things that I learned that would help us on this journey were:[1]

- The vomiting of blood and the passing of black stools and the build up of fluids are all symptoms of end stage liver disease. – Don had all of these

---

1 Liver Pre-Op Teaching Manual – Southern Alberta Transplant Clinic – 5th Floor North Twoer Foothills medical Clinic, 1403 29th Street N.W. Clagary, Alberta, T2N 2T9

- The liver is the largest organ in the body. Weighing 1200 to 1500 grams. It is located on the right side of the abdomen, to the right of the stomach, and behind the lower ribs.
- The livers main functions are to help absorb food and change food into nutrients that the body can use.
- It stores fat, sugars, iron and vitamins for later use in the body.
- It filters the blood to remove substances like drugs, alcohol, and other toxins that are harmful to the body.
- The liver makes proteins needed for normal blood clotting, normal blood pressure, and helping the immune system.

There are sixteen other symptoms of liver disease, some people only have a few of them, my son had ten. There are about one hundred different causes of cirrhosis, but once you have cirrhosis the experience of all sufferers is much the same regardless of the causes. Cirrhosis is the scaring of the liver that makes the liver unable to do any of the jobs it is supposed to do. Cirrhosis leads to problems such as high blood pressure in the veins around the liver, this is called portal hypertension. This high blood pressure is the root cause of vomiting blood from varicose veins in the throat, and the fluid collecting in the belly called ascites.

When the liver is cirrhotic it is very hard and rigid, more like a rock than the sponge it should be. Mental confusion, or encephalopathy can be caused by the failure of the liver to remove ammonia and other toxins from the blood. There is no cure for end stage liver disease, once you have one or more of the end stage symptoms it is time to think about a liver transplant.

October 7, 2004, was the day we drove the hour to the city to have the ultrasound. Don's breathing was labored making this a very hard day. The results of the ultrasound would be back at our local clinic in a few days. We made another appointment with our family doctor. The few short blocks to the doctors office from Don's home was a tense drive. I knew that the news would not be good, all I had to do was look at my son.

When the doctor came into the examining room, our once friendly and warm doctor seemed stern and angered. He held the result sheet in his hand. The ultrasound examination was limited due to patient obesity. A large amount of fluid was present, the liver appeared small and nodular, the spleen was enlarged. This suggested cirrhosis with portal hypertension. After explaining the results any hope of help here seemed to be yanked from our reach. After our doctor had read us the results I understood why he was angry. The results were as he had predicted earlier. We were there in this little room, with the voice of the doctor coming at us like an echo. This is the result he had earlier predicted on one of our emergency room visits, if Don did not quit drinking long before this. Donnie pulled at his pants as he stood up to try to get his belly covered, the shirt would not meet his pants, and the sloppy jogging pants – the only thing he could get on – were twisted and uncomfortable. I could tell that Don was frightened by what he had heard, and he said to me later, "Well I'm dying, I know I am dying." He shuffled out of the room.

I stayed behind, unable to speak for some time. My once strong voice came out in a whisper "Is Don dying?"

The doctor patted me on the back and told me "He has maybe two months to live, it will be a very painful death. Keep him as comfortable as you can. You are a strong person. You can handle it."

I whispered, "Could the fluid be drained to make him more comfortable?"

Sternly the doctor replied "It could, but would immediately fill again."

With that I left to take my dying son home. It was a terrible day. Don was completely fatigued when we arrived back at his home even though it was only a ten minute drive. Getting in and out of the car used up all of his energy. Getting him settled into bed was our next task. I lifted his large legs onto the bed. His back hurt and there was no comfortable position for him to be in. He was freezing, so I began to pile more blankets on him. The weight hurt his shivering body. I had no one to turn to for guidance.

I spent many of the hours of the day at this time with Don, not wanting my Son to be alone. He would fall asleep for just minutes at a time, and on one occasion as he opened his eyes, he said, "Before I open my eyes I fear that I will be alone, then I open them and you are here. I don't know how you do it Mom."

Certainly the doctor was through with us. We were left with little hope. Yes, I realize that Don had not taken his earlier advice to stop abusing his body, but if alcoholism is a sickness why would they give up on a patient now? I questioned myself. I felt abandoned by our family doctor.

This being said I was not ready to give up.

There were other avenues to follow. I was very familiar with alternative therapy and within an hour I had an appointment made at a naturopathic clinic in a nearby city. This lady, that we would see, and who had long been involved with our family, is a scientist and works in natural healing. She understands the medical treatment system. After her testing with Don on October 20, 2004 she felt that there was a very small amount of liver function left. Maybe just enough to get it healthy enough to start to rejuvenate. She was optimistic, and her program for us was intense.

When we arrived home from the appointment I tucked a weakened Don into bed. His Dad and I set out to buy the best juicer possible, then to the grocery store to purchase all of the leafy green vegetables we could find, as prescribed by the naturopath. Don was to drink six ounces of vegetable greens every four hours four times per day. We had the produce manager at our local grocery store order in the greens on the list that we had been given. If we could not get them in our small town we would drive to the nearest cities to get them. It was a steady job preparing this juice, first washing the greens in a special veggie wash to ensure that there were no harmful chemicals on them, juicing, then washing the juicer (which seemed to be a gigantic job). All of this was done in Don's small kitchen so that he would not be alone. Don's system handled the juice pretty well for about four days. He had been troubled with diarrhea prior to beginning this new regime and it got worse as we continued on this stringent new program.

Every moment of every day was a challenge to know if we were really doing the right thing. We knew that we were following the directions of the naturopathic doctor and her previous advice had been useful, but this time it seemed to be very difficult. We shopped, washed, and juiced for five days. Don could no longer hold anything down on his stomach. He spent much of his time in the bathroom. I contacted the naturopathic specialist on the fifth day. I was concerned about Don's well being. She sadly said in a quite voice that she could no longer help us, the treatment she had prescribed was not working as intended and a liver specialist must be our next step.

Our family doctor did not refer us to a specialist, he believed that Don would be gone before he would be able to get an appointment. I had waited and prayed for a long time for a chance to help Don and there was no way that I was going to stop now. Determination, fear, and yes – hope drove me. My list of help was not depleted. I knew a wonderful lady doctor, Doctor Thompson, whom I had been seeing on occasion for some years. She is a medical doctor, but was also treating patients using alternative methods. She knew about my concern for my son as I had discussed him with her on a previous visit. Her father was an alcoholic, and she knew firsthand how devastating it was. She spoke with me gently and caring. I faxed Don's blood work and ultrasound reports to her. After studying them she consulted with her husband, who is a lung specialist, and they called me the same evening.

She said, "I know how much you love your children. Your son is very, very sick."

CHAPTER 4

Making A Decision

"I HAVE TALKED to a doctor in Mexico," I told Doctor Thompson. She replied that she was familiar with this doctors treatment methods. I said, "We are taking Don there in two days."

She advised us to stop at a hospital emergency room where a doctor could see Don and try to get him stabilized so that he could make the trip to Mexico. She feared he would not make the trip if this precaution was not taken.

Every country has its own regulations on medical methods and we are in a fortunate position in our country to be free to consider many options of health care. I already had my mind set on the next option we would consider. I considered the long waits that often seemed to plague emergency rooms and decided that we must start preparing to go straight to San Diego.

I was searching for a way to improve Don's general health which was failing fast. I certainly understood that the liver was barely functioning and that this was causing major problems for his body, but needed to take him where we could get help to keep him alive long enough to make the necessary arrangements for him to see a liver specialist. In my frightened opinion this was my only hope at this time.

San Diego was the entrance point for our medical treatment in Mexico. Dr. Castillo in Tijuana was a special friend of ours. Twenty-two years previous we had been to him with my sister-in-law who was choosing alternative care for cancer. At that time he had just opened his clinic and was not terribly busy, so we would go for supper with him after the clinic closed and visit with him on a personal level. He had been to our town to give a lecture on his alternative treatment methods. In the past twenty-two years we had been to his clinic three times, once for my own health, the other times with relatives who were suffering.

When I spoke to this fine Mexican doctor he said, "Bring your son here as quick as possible."

The clinic had grown from the small office he had started with, to a large, modern, and beautiful clinic, just inside the Mexican border in the city of Tijuana. Dr. Castillo had received his medical training in the United States and early in his career made a decision to practice in Mexico where the law allowed him to incorporate both traditional and alternative methods.

God was unfolding a plan for us that we worked quickly to put in place. On Tuesday night my husband and I knew that Mexico was our only choice. Don was failing fast. He could barely turn over on the bed without help. He laboured to breath as fluid surrounded his lungs. It was impossible for Don's Dad to leave his job at this time as he had no one to take over for him as the head of our family business. I assured my husband that I could do this, and I was determined I was going to. We called our other children that evening and told them of our plans. Instantly one of our daughters told us she was coming with us, even though this meant she would be away from her own busy family and business. Our other daughter offered to take care of things at our home, and her brother's. Lists were made and tickets were bought for an eleven o'clock flight departing Thursday morning. By Wednesday afternoon the lists were getting shorter, laundry was done, bags were packed, calls were placed to cancel appointments and rearrange our other commitments. We accomplished in one day what would often take people a week to do under more regular circumstances.

About three o'clock Wednesday afternoon I thought about something Don had said to me months earlier. We had offered to take Don to the clinic in Mexico before he had decided to quit drinking. At that time he declined our offer, we had hoped that it would be a chance for him to have a change of scenery, and an opportunity to become healthier, in hopes that he would give up drinking. At that time he said something to the effect of – he didn't even know if he could get across the line (Canada/ U.S.A. border). Because he declined to go we didn't even explore this problem any further. Panic came over me – What had he meant? I had to figure out a way to find out if there could be a problem going through customs. This could not be one of those wait and see cases, my son's life hung in the balance. My daughter and I discussed it, and decided that I should go to the police station to see if they could help me. We live in a small town and I knew the person at the front desk of the police office. I explained our situation and was told that he would be able to check Don's records, but would be unable to tell me what they contained, but he could advise me whether we would have problems crossing international borders after reviewing the results. He advised me that it was a possibility that we could encounter difficulty crossing the border. We did not tell Donnie about this, I was afraid it would be an unnecessary worry given his current concern over the trip. I called customs at the airport from which we would depart. The compassionate customs officer put Don's name into the computer and said that if they checked he would be stopped and prevented from leaving Canada. I had not shed tears in the past months, but they flowed freely as I explained the matter of life and death I was facing with my son. The agent spoke to his supervisor and they said by all means they would ensure passage for my son on this trip only. They gave me their names and assured me they would be there to see that we got on our plane. It turned out that the blemish that would impede Don from crossing the border was an incident from when he was nineteen and had had a small scuffle with another person. They advised me to have Don get a pardon (which he has since done). Another hurdle was passed as the evening drew near.

I checked my list to see how we were progressing on the things that I knew had to be done. I was not through yet ! The customs officer had told me to bring a letter from our doctor stating that Don was crossing the border for health reasons. Now I had to ask our family doctor for a letter. I braced myself for this task and slipped over to the doctors office. His receptionist fit me in between patients. Our doctor was aware of the fact that members of our family, as well as other people from our town had been to this clinic in Mexico. He agreed to prepare the letter that I required, advising us that we were wasting our money. He told me I could pick the letter up at the hospital desk after eight o'clock that evening. I appreciated this as I knew that this was not something that he would ordinarily do.

The next issue that presented itself was that Don decided that he should have a will before we left for Mexico. He struggled to get out of bed, I don't know where he found his strength. His mind was somewhat confused with the anxiety that the journey presented. I got Don a will template from the stationary store, and he proceeded to fill it out, and then called his brother-in-law to witness it. This added to the emotional stress of the time, but I realized then that Don was facing the facts. We did not know the outcome of this trip that we were facing.

November 3, 2004, was drawing to a close, it was after ten in the evening when Don finished his will and I got him settled into bed. It had been a busy twelve hours of preparation for this journey. We were anticipating what seemed to be our best option at the time, in hopes that Don would become well enough to access medical treatment back at home. As I gently lifted first his left leg then his right leg into the bed fear once again made my hands tremble. In my heart was a prayer, Dear God, we must get Don to Mexico. I rubbed his aching back with a soothing, cool rub and tucked him into bed under warm blankets. He was shivering and so uncomfortable. The fluid in his belly was steadily increasing. Once again, I wanted to stay with him, but Don said "Mom, go home you need some rest."

Our plane left at eleven o'clock the next morning, and we needed to leave our home by 7:00 a.m. How was Don ever going to survive this I wondered to myself. One difficulty that I had not crossed off of my list had to be dealt with that morning – Don had pretty well lost control of his bowels, and bladder. I had purchased a package of disposable men's undergarments, and I worried how he would accept this. Ever since Don had quit drinking and realized his life was in danger he never once disagreed or fought anything he needed to do, he was fighting to live, he wanted a second chance. He met this challenge with the same perseverance and willingness.

The morning of our departure was rushed, I awoke early, I knew that Don would be awake as he found it hard to sleep. How could he possibly sleep when he knew the day we had ahead of us? Our granddaughter was driving us to the airport. Don's Dad and I put our well packed suitcases in the vehicle and left our small town behind us. We were on a mission, a mission that just had to succeed.

Don had decided that he would not even try to eat or drink on the flight. He felt that this would be best for traveling. We had taken along a couple of protein bars for him if he needed them. He had not been able to eat for a couple of days, and his body was very weak. There were some quick tearful goodbyes as we picked up my daughter at her home, on our way to the airport. My granddaughter and her mother were in the front seat, and Don and I were in the back. Don's Dad was trying hard to hold back the tears in his eyes, as he watched his wife, daughter, and son set out on this search for life. He worried about what would happen.

Don laid his head back and barely said a word on the hour-and-a-half trip to the airport. My granddaughter dropped us off at the airlines door, our daughter rushed to get a cart. Don slowly inched his way out of the truck. His feet could barely carry his legs, and his legs could barely carry his body. He would not let me get a wheelchair for him. We said goodbye to our granddaughter and made our way into the huge airport. At that moment a sense of overwhelming gratitude for Don's sister came over me. Yes, I would have managed I am sure, but now my daughter took over. All Don and I had to do was whatever she told us to. "Go this way Mom, follow me", those words were music to my ears.

Going through customs went well, a customs officer took us through quickly. No words were spoken, but when our eyes met I knew who he was, and it certainly was not hard for him to know that I was the desperate mom he had spoken to yesterday afternoon. I thanked him quietly, as I touched his arm, there really are angels everywhere. Soon we were in the terminal, we had an hour to wait before the plane left. Thankfully it was on time. We had two seats together and one a couple of rows behind. Don and I took the two seats together, with Don in the aisle seat, this gave him a little extra room. His body filled the seat and his legs were swelling more, as they did when he was sitting or walking. We were ten hours away from a bed for my son to rest on and I wondered how we would ever make it. My daughter and I were praying silently – please dear God help us get Don to this wonderful caring doctor. Don sat still, never moving and breathing heavily. His eyes protruded and stared straight ahead. Don does not remember the flight to San Diego, it is probably best this way, but his sister and I certainly do.

CHAPTER 5

The Next Three Weeks

We arrived in San Diego about five in the evening, Don inched his way out of the plane and hung onto the luggage cart. We had been given a phone number for the shuttle bus company that the clinic used. We called them and stood by the airport door anxiously waiting. We were all tired.

The clinic had ongoing arrangements with two motels just on the American side of the Mexican border for its patients and their families. A shuttle bus drove patients to and from the clinic, just inside of Mexico, six days of the week, taking all of the stress out of continually crossing the border. The clinic worked six days of the week to accommodate their patients from around the world; and did everything possible to make their stay as comfortable, and pleasant as circumstances would allow. We arrived at the motel about seven thirty in the evening, it was a beautiful evening. After paying the bus driver and receiving their card, we checked into the motel. The next half hour was spent getting Don up the outside flight of stairs to the room. We had two rooms booked side by side. This had been a thirteen hour day for us, to Don it must have seemed like an eternity. Don steadied and pulled himself up using the railing on the stairs, step, by, step, with minutes in between each painful step. I encouraged him by saying "Just a few more steps Donnie." He appeared not to hear me. Sandra had rushed ahead to open the doors to the rooms. She made three trips back to drag our luggage into our rooms. The lady at the desk had offered to help, but like the little train that could, we knew we could, we knew we could, and we were just about there, only a few hours and Don would be in the hands of Dr. Castillo.

Don had his own room with a queen size bed and a large comfortable chair and footstool. The room had a little kitchen area, and the bath had a tub and shower. It was nothing fancy, but it looked good to us, and would be our home for the next three weeks. My daughter busied herself in our room, getting us settled, while I stayed in Don's room helping him to get settled. He sat on the edge of the bed as I carefully took off his shirt. I slowly pulled off his jogging pants, each leg was so heavy, it was all I could do to lift them one at a time onto the bed. Don's chest was rattling with fluid, and he could barely breathe. I fluffed and placed pillows under his head to keep him in a upright position, he hurt all over.

There was a Denny's restaurant just next to our motel. Don's sister had slipped over and brought soup and crackers back for him. I helped Don eat a little soup. After going over instructions on how to call the front office, or to dial my room number, Sandra and I settled into our room. I clutched the key to Don's room in my hand. Don was in God's hands for the night. We prayed for sleep to come not only for Don, but for us as well.

We woke early Friday morning to catch the shuttle bus. Sandra and I were excited about the bus ride, we had both experienced it before. The driver Raul made this an unforgettable part of the stay. He was a short wiry, Mexican, with a cheerful personality, like no one else we had ever known. He tried to make you forget why you were there. He made you laugh when you may have wanted to cry. He called you beautiful, my friend, my brothe', my siste', put his arm around you, and ran to help all he could, or would say "wai' here my frien', I be right there. He directed the seating so that those who were the sickest, or the least able to get out were near the front. He was truly one of God's servants, he had been running the shuttle bus for twenty-five years, and could not retire because of his love for people, and his desire to help. His 'God bless you my friend' touched the hearts of all that he met, even those who didn't know that God was there to bless us.

Raul recognized Sandra and I from our previous visits to the clinic and was delighted to see us. When he saw my son he came to him and said, "God bless you my son! Just stay here – you be my co-pilot today, I get you to the clinica quickly." Being Raul's co-pilot meant that you sat in the front seat, and were the first one off of the shuttle. Raul made the trip across the border ten to fifteen times per day. He laughed and joked with the Mexican custom officers as they waved us through; a bus load of sick people and their supporters. At times there were patients who arrived alone for their treatment, soon they too were absorbed into this clinic family. Don was in the co-pilots seat but was unable to respond to Raul. Raul watched him as he talked and drove. "My friend stay with me, I just two corners, and I be there." Needless to say, both the sick and the healthy hung on for dear life as we screeched down the road to the clinic. When Raul stopped in front of the clinic he turned and said, "Please wai' one Mexican minute, I get my friend to the doctor, then I help you beautiful people." How could one not feel lifted in such a positive atmosphere?

Raul had phoned ahead of our arrival for a wheelchair for Don, and took him into the doctors office as soon as we arrived. Dr. Castillo helped Don onto one of only two beds in the clinic. He called for another doctor. Dr. Rubio came quickly. He told the nurse to get the lab technician to take blood, and rapidly set up an IV. Within the first half hour blood was taken and the IV successfully started and Dr. Rubio was preparing to drain some fluid from Don's abdominal cavity. I had brought all of the blood and ultrasound tests from our previous medical visits with us on the trip. Dr. Costillo was studying them and sharing the information from them with the other doctors and nurses. Don was finally in Dr. Costillo's Clinic, with the doctor that we had so much faith and trust in for this part of the healing process. Moments after Don was settled Dr. Costillo turned to greet Sandra and I with a huge hug, and expressed that he was so glad that we had brought Don to the clinic, and promised to help him. The warmth of his embrace and his kind manner brought tears to our eyes. Our lips once again uttered a thankful prayer, with the help of God and Don's strong determination we had made the journey. We had been advised that Don should fast in order to begin the blood work upon our arrival, this was no problem as Don had not eaten for a few days.

The I.M.O.Q. Clinic, as I mentioned before, is located just across the Mexican border from San Ysidro, California. Some of the family members that are accompanying their loved ones to the clinic often walk from the motel to the clinic, it took about twenty minutes in twenty degree sunshine, not hard to take on a November day. Later on in our stay Sandra walked with new friends, while I rode the bus with Don. The clinic is a day clinic which opens at 8:00 a.m. and closes around five or six in the evening, whatever is required to see all of the patients. It is a modern health facility with state of the art equipment. They have a professional staff, and their goal is to improve health by focusing on the patient and treating the cause of the disease, rather than just the symptoms. They use advanced natural therapies which are recognized around the world, that cleanse the body and build the immune system. The clinic has their own pharmacy, x-ray and ultrasound equipment, laboratory, and a dentist. They have one room with two beds, Don occupied one of these beds for the twenty-one days that we were there. This room was adjacent to the nurses station. The first visit for all new patients is twenty-one days. Others come for check-ups or booster treatments which last between three and ten days. All patients are treated using intravenous supplements. They are seated in comfortable chairs in a large open room, there are about twenty-five chairs in all, five of them are reclining chairs for those who are to sick too sit up for the length of the treatment.

I was overcome with relief and gratitude as I stood back

in the tiny room where Don lay, and watched the doctors move quickly and confidently to save my son. Other patients were hopeful and felt blessed to be in the clinic receiving this alternative therapy. As I moved my eyes from one person to another I knew that this was going to be a special experience for all who were there. There then seemed to be time for Sandra and I to leave Don's small room for the larger space in the clinic to collect our thoughts.

As you step into the clinic you find yourself in a spotless waiting room with the pharmacy, lab, and diagnostic room opening from the main reception area. There is a small kitchen area which has a refrigerator, sink, and microwave for everyone to use. There are tables and chairs so you can bring your lunch or have a cup of tea and visit with other people who are there. New patients can expect to be at the clinic for about five hours on their first day, this includes blood work, all examinations, and a thorough visit with a doctor in the morning, usually by noon they have begun an intravenous treatment. At the end of the day they meet with the doctor again to review their test results and at that time they will review the schedule of treatment that the doctors prescribe, including blood tests, and necessary lab work and doctor appointments every five days or sooner according to individual requirements.

I clutched a cup of hot tea in my hand as I slowly walked around this marvellous clinic. As I moved into the large treatment room I saw all of the patients getting settled into their chairs to receive their treatments. People were talking, sharing stories of their illnesses, and of how they found out about this clinic. Others were there with great success stories accompanying family members or friends who were in search of healing. Many had cancer, some hepatitis C, some diabetes, some heart problems, undiagnosed infections like e-coli, and others. I stood in awe, hardly able to believe that we were there. I silently thanked God that we were fortunate enough to know about this place, and able to make the trip safely. This type of treatment is not covered by our medical system, we felt fortunate to be able to provide this care for our son, and trusted that God would lead the way.

My tea needed to be warmed, I had held it too long as I looked around thinking and praying for all of the people who surrounded me. I went back to the kitchen area to find Sandra and her new friends sharing and laughing together. You become part of the family when you are in this place, you come to care for all who are there, and offer them your prayers and hope. The bond becomes very strong, and you are never alone, there is no personal struggle, it becomes shared. All who saw Raul wheel Donnie in already cared about him and they didn't even know our story. Many people at home were praying for Don, but those who saw his swollen body as he entered the clinic also held prayers in their hearts for him. One of the many noticeable characteristics of this clinic was that the staff and doctors were not afraid to say "God bless you" or "I'll pray for you", this was contagious, even for those patients who were often not so vocal with this type of sentiment.

Now it was time to step back into Don's little room to check on how he was doing. This was the first time in a long while that fear did not overwhelm me. Dr. Rubio was leaning over a restful looking Don as a tube ran from his abdominal area to a large bottle on the floor. In total they would drain six quarts of fluid (imagine 2 large, two litre milk bottles full) from Don's abdomen that day. An IV was in his arm with two bottles of treatment attached. It was at that time that Don opened his eyes, and a smile crept onto his face. Don later told me that he did not remember anything about our flight to Mexico, the evening in the hotel, or his drive with Raul to the clinic. His first memory was when he opened his eyes to see a Mexican person leaning over him. He then realized that we had reached our destination.

Early in the afternoon Dr. Castillo called me into his office. Sandra and I listened to the results of the tests, it was too much for one person to absorb. Don had severe inflammation of the liver, his immune system was extremely weak, he was anemic, had infection, parasites, and his kidney function was dangerously low, he was malnourished, his heart was laying side-ways in his chest because of all the fluid, and only a small portion of his liver was functioning. Dr. Costillo hoped that this treatment would help the small portion of the liver rejuvenate. The IV treatments and fluid draining took seven hours that first day. At the end of our first day Don was able to slowly walk to the bus without the wheel chair. Raul placed him in the co-pilots seat and joked with him for the entire ride. "My co-pilot, he much better now, bless you my son, thank you for taking us to clinic t'is morning." He asked everyone on the bus to give him a big thank-you, everyone was encouraging us as a loud round of applause filled the bus.

When we arrived back at our rooms Don slowly climbed the stairs, and once again I tucked him into bed, he was exhausted. With six quarts of fluid removed from his abdominal cavity, his body moved, just a little easier. We had a steep hill to climb, but Don seemed to have the determination to take on the challenge. Supper for Don was another bowl of Denny's soup, though he was not hungry. One of his IV's that day had been vitamin and mineral therapy, I am sure it helped Don, and it certainly made me feel better knowing that he was getting some nourishment.

About seven o'clock that evening, when Don was settled in and watching a television show from his bed, Sandra and I went to Denny's for some supper. Even though we rushed through our meal it was a nice break. We took the kitchen dishes out of Don's room and added them to our small kitchen suite, so that we could cook our own breakfast and supper. We would also pack a lunch to take with us to the clinic. We knew that our days there would be long. The treatment program that Dr. Costillo gave us for Don would take seven hours each day.

A man in his forties shared the small room with Don, he was suffering from cancer caused by asbestos. His wife and Sandra became friends, they walked to a nearby market to get things that they seemed to think were necessary! A walk in the beautiful wind free country with the warm weather made everyone want to be outside. They were the 'go-getters' for everyone in the clinic. Each day we would watch through the waiting room window waiting for the fresh fruit stand to be set up. Soon there would be a line up of people to buy their plate of freshly cut up fruit, to us this was quite a novelty.

Each Tuesday and Friday a bus left the motel at five in the evening to take clinic patients or their support people to the health food and grocery stores. Sandra left the clinic by noon on those days and kept our small kitchenette fridge well stocked. She also prepared this food so that we had good things to eat each day – what would Don and I have done without her? I needed to be at the clinic all of the time with Don in case something happened. Even though I was not the one to help him, the doctors were there for Don's every need, and the nurses watched him as they went about caring for others. Each day during those twenty one days was filled with emotion. Everyone that saw Don could not believe how sick he was and the struggle that he was willing to endure to keep going.

The IV treatments that Don was receiving daily were:

- Chelation (an intravenous injection of a man-made amino acid that cleanses the arteries, and rejuvenates the cardio-vascular system)
- Iron
- Multi-vitamins and minerals
- Live liver cells
- Anti-inflammatory
- and a treatment to rid his body from parasites.

Most days he would be given three of the five. Blood tests were taken regularly, after seeing the results the doctor would add anything that he felt would be beneficial to Don. Fluid filled Don's body almost as soon as it was drained. Dr. Rubio "tapped"(using a needle and a tube to drain the fluid from the abdominal cavity) him every two to three days. One of the functions of the liver is to produce, the protein albumin. Albumin performs many functions, including maintaining the "Osmotic pressure" that causes fluid to remain within the blood stream, instead of leaking out into the tissues. Liver disease and kidney disease and malnutrition are major causes of low albumin. If albumin gets very low swelling can occur in the ankles, legs, and accumulate in the legs and abdomen. If the person does not return to health, as in Don's case with cirrhosis of the liver, the only way to correct the albumin is to have a liver transplant. The clinic hoped to turn Don's health around so that the liver could do its job.

On the eighth day Don's blood tests showed that the albumin levels were dangerously low. Doctors ordered albumin for him immediately. This treatment was not available in the clinics pharmacy so they brought it in, what I mean by this is a Mexican boy jumped on his bicycle with my one hundred dollar American bill in his hand to pick it up from their main pharmacy. As I watched him leave he was weaving in and out of honking traffic, creating a scene that still scares me. Don was in a crisis. Doctors were working at his side giving him life saving attention. The lab technician was taking blood and getting the results back to the medical team quickly. I stood in the tiny room with my heart pounding. My thoughts flashed back over the past few months and all we had been through to get to this point. Dr. Costillo came and put his arms around me assuring me it would be okay that Don only needed albumin. Just as he spoke the messenger rushed in with a little parcel that would mean life for my son. The nurses ran the bottle under warm water to get the substance to room temperature. Doctor Rubio was reaching out for it and quickly attaching it to the IV and dripping life into Don's body. Color slowly began to creep back into

Don's yellowed face and his eyes started to focus and I felt the fear begin to leave my body and soul. What if we hadn't been there? What if the doctors had not been right there? All of these what if's sprang into my mind. I knew at that time that Don would have slipped away if we had not been at the clinic. This treatment rallied Don surprisingly quickly, not that he was 100% better, but he was at the improved state that we had seen earlier in the day. He definitely was a bit stronger. The past few evenings at supper time he would come into the room that Sandra and I shared, we called it the dining room, and sit at our little table to eat the healthy supper that Sandra had prepared. We visited for a half hour or so, we usually had phone calls from home through out the evening and we would visit with family and the hear about the goings on of our small town. Don was soon ready to make his way back to his own room, and perhaps would even watch a television show while he rested in bed.

Don had fluid drained from his body approximately six times while we were at the clinic. This gave him relief, but invariably the fluid would return to his abdominal cavity. Each day the treatments continued, as Don lay on his back, not moving and looking straight ahead. What must he be thinking I wondered? He stayed calm, not too anxious to talk, and certainly not wanting to visit. We would bring him small dishes of freshly cut fruit or a chocolate bar. It was as if he thought, well here I am please do whatever it takes. Don was pleasant and accommodating, he was frightened, but his will stayed strong.

The next few days at the clinic went along fairly smoothly. Sandra and I each had check-ups while we were there, as well as a series of cheleation therapies. We sat with the others in the large treatment room, visiting, getting to know everyone who was attending the clinic. Some days Sandra went back to the motel after lunch to run errands, to keep our "home" running smoothly. Luckily there was a beautiful shopping centre three blocks away. When Don was having a better early evening, Sandra and I would go to the shopping centre and buy a garment or two... We were there on Black Friday, the day following American Thanksgiving, and the kick off for Christmas. On that special day Sandra and I had left at 6:00 A.M. and rushed to the stores that had opened at 4:00 A.M., only to stand in a long line outside to buy sweaters we had picked out the day before. What a way to get early Christmas shopping done – 70% off at Tommy Hilfiger- sounds too good to be true! As we watched the time in the checkout line with our arms and shopping bags loaded we realized that it was time to go back and get Don ready for the bus and off to the clinic. After a quick discussion I was elected to stand in the snake like line with far more goods than I could handle and Sandra hustled off to the motel. I was to catch the next shuttle bus over to the clinic – after I had returned to the motel with our purchases. Sandra got Don organized and outside waiting for the bus. It was at that time that Don shared his thoughts on our early morning escapade (He had known we were going). He firmly sent Sandra back to rescue me and assured Sandra that he could go to the clinic without us but that his Mother could not be left alone in the shopping centre. Sandra got back to the locked door of the store, where security guards would only let ten people in and out at a time, this meant that Sandra was at the back of the line again. She stood there for a moment, then taking a chance, with people glaring at her, she went to talk to the security guard. She explained her need to get back into the store to help me, she could see my white hair and pointed me out to the guard. Everyone else in the store was much darker skinned than I as we were in a Mexican neighbourhood. He had remembered noticing my white hair when we arrived, and he let Sandra in to help me.

That first evening in San Ysidro while Sandra and I were in our P.J.'s propped up on our pillows sipping tea, we thought here we are – a mom and two of her kids, let's make this as special as possible, as well as a healing trip, we did just that.

Our lives fell into a routine, and I became more relaxed as I could see strength creeping its way into Don's body. I was filled with continued hope and did not hesitate to thank God for this blessing. The morning of the twelfth day that we were at the clinic the procedure was the same as the previous days. Don entered the clinic and took his place in the little room, still anxious to be on the bed for the day. He had his IV treatments and was having more fluid drained in the afternoon, which could take up to two hours. Four quarts were siphoned out of his abdominal cavity. When we got back to the motel, Don was worn out from the short trip. He remarked that he was freezing, which seemed impossible to others, as the weather seemed so warm, even hot to some. Once again I piled on the extra blankets. Sandra was busy in the kitchenette cooking brown rice and fresh fish for supper. I sat with Don until he seemed to relax, it had been a hard day. Sandra and I enjoyed our supper, but Don only ate a small amount.

Six o'clock came and Don said, "Mom I am ready to get settled in," thus beginning our evening ritual.

As I lifted his legs into bed and rubbed his tired back I felt how warm his body was, yet he said he was freezing. My mind flashed back to when my kids were little and were coming down with something. I slipped into my room to discuss this with Sandra. We had failed to get an after hours number for the doctors, how foolish of us when Don was so sick. By eight o'clock Don was burning with fever, I wrung out large bath towels in cool water and covered him. We had to keep the fever down. Sandra helped until eleven o'clock when I felt that I could handle Don on my own. Sandra went back to our room to rest and pray, Don's room key held in her hand. She crept into Don's room continually to check on Don and I to see how we were doing, as I continued to try to keep Don cool and bring down the fever. I would not let her take over, I needed to be there. Don would rest for a few minutes then be awake, but not very alert. This frightened me even more, and we continued to pray. At four o'clock A.M. Don's fever broke. I covered him gently and lay down beside him. The next time that Sandra came in I was sleeping, and not too quietly from what I understand.

Don whispered to Sandra, "Don't disturb Mom, I'll just stay awake and listen to the snoring."

I awoke at seven in the morning to find that Don was very sick and very weak. The bus came at nine, we had two hours to keep him going. Sandra brought in a little breakfast. I ate mine, as I was well aware of the day I would have before me. Don drank a few sips of juice. We were all very tired. We needed to get to the clinic as soon as possible. I went into my room to get ready for the day, while Sandra busily packed our lunch. Fifteen minutes later I returned to Don's room to help him get dressed. I spoke to him gently and asked him to move his legs over to the side of the bed. "I'll help you lift them down." I said.

Don replied in a whisper, "Mom, I can't go to the clinic today. I just can't make it."

On hearing that I stood firmly and said "Don, you are going, if Sandra and I have to carry you, we are going to get you there."

Sandra came into the room and together we got the very weak Don dressed and ready to get on the bus. We left the room long before our nine o'clock bus was due. It was going to take time to navigate the stairs. We prayed that Raul and the other patients would be early.

When Raul arrived he rushed out to help get Don on the bus. Raul looked frightened as he knew that this was going to be another critical trip into Tijuana. The passengers were hurried onto the bus, each moving quietly and as swiftly as they were able. The ride to the clinic was not the usual good morning chatter. Today was different. Raul, as he had on the first morning, kept taking to Don. "My friend, stay with me, my brother, stay with me." Again Raul called ahead for a wheelchair and help to meet us upon our arrival. The doctors had an IV set up and a lab technician ready to take blood, both doctors were present, this was a serious situation. The clinic was quiet as they worked over Don, the blood work was done and the results came fast. Don's albumin level had become dangerously low. This was causing his liver to fail. He needed more albumin, the young Mexican man once again jumped on his bicycle and set off racing to get the life saving albumin, not even waiting for me to give him the hundred dollars, this was a crisis. I knew that each patient that had once again seen Don wheeled into the clinic or on the bus had a prayer for him on their lips, and the two wonderful Mexican nurses were saying ,"Don we pray for you."

Sandra and I stood speechless as the doctors added yet another IV to the one all ready dripping into Don's body. To me it seemed forever, but in actuality it was only about fifteen minutes before the albumin was in the nurses hands and being prepared for the IV. After the IV was feeding the albumin into Don's body the doctor stepped back and turned to Sandra and I and said, "Don improve soon."

This was another one of the miracles of our body, if given the right treatment whether it be medical, the food we eat, or holistic, it will fight to become healthy once again. In less than an hour Don had colour returning to his yellow cheeks and we had made it past another crisis. I think of a chapter in the Bible where Luke reminds us of the realities of life's difficulties. But then encourages those living in crisis to hold on to Christ. Life is real, God's love is real, Both are to be shared and the love feeds the endurance. I never lost hope.

The rest of the day went well and Don managed to sleep a little, as his daily treatment continued. Sandra and I sat in the waiting room, heads bobbing, as we caught moments of shut-eye. Part of the alternative treatment for the liver was eating sugar cane and drinking pure Welshes Grape Juice. This recommendation sent Sandra and her friend off to the Mexican market a few blocks away to buy raw sugar cane. We bought and took the grape juice with us each day, as we passed from the U.S.A. into Mexico. Don's new "favourite" food became sugar cane. He ate all he possibly could and drank grape juice like water. This regime was to cleanse the toxins from his liver, the grape juice to cleanse, and the sugar cane to heal.

Dr. Rubio "tapped" the fluid from Don's body. He is a very quiet and compassionate man, and he made you feel as if you were the only patient he had. As he gave Don his treatments he spoke gently even though it was often a one sided conversation. The kind doctor offered Don personal support and encouragement. When Dr. Rubio learned that Don's occupation was in construction he told Don about the house he was planning to build on a hill. Dr. Rubio asked Don many questions and for his advice on many construction related matters, all the time trying to draw Don out of his pain and into a world that he knew and enjoyed. The subject that the doctor gently alluded to in his treatment of Don was that he was not alone in his struggle.

One day Doctor Rubio told Don the story of his own brother as he worked, he said, "My br'ther he drank, and drank, and drank. And Oh my M'ther she so sad, she worry and cries, and nothing she can do. My M'ther so sad. So one day I buy the largest bottle of tequila I can find and go my brother's house. I plunk it down on the floor and say I bring you a present. My br'ther he was so shocked and said you are a doctor why you not help me? I said I am helping you. You want to die, I'll help you die quickly. Drink this it make it faster. My br'ther he was quiet for a Mexican minute. Take it away he telled me – I want to live." Dr. Rubio then continued to tell how he took the bottle of tequila back to the car and brought in a large cane of sugar for his brother. Dr. Rubio's brother now grows sugar cane to help others who are struggling to overcome the disease of alcoholism. "Now my

M'ther she is so happy , she is so happy." Dr. Rubio was on a mission to build up Don's self-esteem, and help him heal emotionally as well as physically, to prepare him for the journey ahead.

The days passed and the treatment and care continued. Sandra and I spent our days visiting others and eating fresh fruit! We were happy that Don was doing better, and now had more time for real visiting with some of the other families who were also at the clinic. Sandra struck up a conversation with a woman from British Columbia and soon found out that she was from the same town as where Sandra's husband had been raised. The two talked a little longer, and soon realized that Sandra's husband had been childhood friends with both this woman and her husband. What a small world it is.

I was chatting with a new family who had arrived at the clinic, and I found that the Mother was a friend of my sisters in Ontario. Dr. Costillo's clinic was known around the world, and it was becoming more and more apparent every day how closely people are connected from around this great world, here in a small Mexican town where all of us were far from home.

On the fifteenth of November 2004, it was Don's Fifty-second birthday. The nurses brought him a cupcake with a candle on it, and even though Don was in another room a loud chorus of happy birthday rang out from the other patients who were there receiving treatment. That was the kind of wonderful people we were surrounded by in this extraordinary clinic.

The last few days at the clinic, we were all thinking more about home and were anxious to return. Kathy, my daughter at home, made sure that we heard all of the news from our small town. She called each evening to fill us in on the latest, and encourage us and keep our spirits high. Don was feeling much stronger, his fluid retention levels were significantly lowered, he was now able to walk, and his colouring was returning to normal. Our emotions were on a roller coaster, high when we thought of getting home, and low when we thought about leaving the safe cocoon that surrounded us at the clinic. We would no longer have a doctor at Don's side, blood tests readily available at all times, or friends supporting us ten hours per day. I wondered nervously how we were going to cope.

The first thing that I had to do upon arriving home was to get Don established with a medical doctor who would be able to care for him. We were taking albumin home, and Dr. Costillo had given us the name of a naturopath that would be able to administer it for us. The last visit with Dr. Costillo was on the twentieth of November, the report on Don's liver said that it was showing slight signs of improvement, but did not confirm that it was healthy enough to rejuvenate itself. Don's general health was greatly renewed. We were extremely satisfied with the progress that had been made in the past twenty-one days. We also knew that this was not the end of our journey, and we left Mexico with renewed hope and determination to continue to fight. Don was now well enough to give us time to find a doctor and do whatever it took to save his life. The last day at the clinic was busy and confusing for Sandra and I as we rushed to get the vitamins, medication, and instructions we were to follow to continue Don's care. By five o'clock in the afternoon we had it under control, this was the first day that Don had not been in bed. He was able to move around, pushing the IV stand as long as there was a chair close by. When he had the last IV removed he went to the foyer of the clinic to wait with the rest of us for Raul. It was time now, for Sandra and I to say our tearful goodbye's. Don was sitting quietly observing everyone, when Emily, a nurse, came running toward him, she said, "Don, Don you are not leaving without saying goodbye!" Emily had her arms outstretched as she said, "God bless you Don!"

Don stood up and put his arms around this wonderful, small, Mexican nurse and said, "And God bless you Emily!" This was a moment for me to remember.

That evening, back at the motel, was spent trying to stuff everything Sandra and I had purchased, not only into the suitcases we had brought, but also the luggage that we had to buy. Sandra decided that if we rolled everything we could get more into a suitcase. We lifted, guessed weight, shuffled, squeezed, jumped on, and anything else we could think of to get suitcases closed and locked. Sandra made lists and gathered receipts for customs. Don had his list for his suitcase, which consisted of Sandra's new wardrobe – plus his two pairs of jogging pants and a couple of shirts.

At last we were ready to roll, at 5 a.m. our taxi was arriving to take us to the airport on time. Twenty-three days after leaving Calgary we were headed home. The flight home was great. Don was able to move around the airport some, and if he got out of my sight I did not panic, it was as if on the trip he had moved from the small toddler stage where his mother worried about him all of the time, to being a teenager capable of managing himself without my shadow overtop of him. I am sure he was relieved.

I think we were all running on adrenaline as we went through customs, who did not even check a thing we had purchased, after all of our lists and organizing! Our family was waiting just past customs at the airport. They were filled with anticipation as they waited for us to appear. I went through, then Sandra, then Don, when he stepped through the door, they could not believe their eyes. The son my husband has sent to Mexico returned many pounds lighter, was walking, and had colour in his face.

We returned home late in the evening. Don was anxious to return to his own bed. He settled himself in that night, and I anxiously returned home as well, happy to be back in my own surroundings.

CHAPTER 6

The Journey Continues

THE MONTH of December, 2004, was filled with family gatherings, and Christmas dinner at our place, Don too was at our dinner table, along with his brother and sisters and their families, a great Christmas present for all of us. As I looked around my dining room table I was overcome with joy and thankfulness.

We welcomed in the New Year – 2005, I had placed a call to Dr. Thompson's office. I was devastated when her receptionist informed me that they were no longer taking new patients. I wondered if she did not remember that I was a patient of there's already. Once again I felt I was left searching for help, and wondering where I would turn. I knew I certainly could not return to the doctor who had sent Don home to die. During the next week I made phone calls to several doctors offices in search of one who would care for my son. I was aware of how busy doctors are and this became even more clear to me now. I knew in my heart that I wanted Dr. Thompson. I prayed as I dialled her number once again. This time I explained in lengthy detail how urgent it was that Don get an appointment with her. The receptionist left the phone and spoke with the doctor. The receptionist did not know that we had been in contact with the doctor earlier. We set an appointment for February 16, 2005, she would be glad to see my son. If you ever doubted God's plan you would know now that His plan was guiding us.

On our first visit with Dr. Thompson she studied the reports and spoke gently to Don as she examined him. She told Don that she understood the disease of alcoholism, as her Dad was an alcoholic and continued to drink until the last few years of his life. In her professional manner, she told of the wonderful man her father became after he put alcohol behind him. Her Dad had many health problems the last few years of his life as a result of his drinking. Dr. Thompson asked Don "Are you ready for this journey?" She assured him that there would be many people who would be willing to help him, as long as he was willing to do his part. It was very obvious that Don's time had come. He was determined to change his lifestyle. Don was reaching out to all of the wonderful people who were there to help mend his broken body. Dr. Thompson told Don, "I have seen the sadness in your mother's eyes when she has come to see me in the past." Don looked to the floor, with remorse for the pain he had caused me.

The first appointment in February 2005 was for an ultrasound of Don's liver. Don was not carrying fluid at this time, and as such a very clear view of the liver could be obtained. Entering this appointment with Don in seemingly good health we had every reason to believe that he was doing well. We knew that the liver was capable of rejuvenating, and that healing was possible. After all we reasoned, Don was now able to work short days, laying patio blocks for his sister, Sandra, and could come and go as his health allowed. After a couple of weeks, before the scheduled ultrasound, Don became short of breath, and some fluid seemed to be collecting around his lungs. This was frightening.

Don always got up early in the morning and went to work for a few hours, he was determined to complete the patio, despite his health challenges. He usually needed a rest after lunch, then he could return to cutting and placing the patio blocks into a perfect pattern for the remainder of the afternoon. At times I thought the work was too hard for him, but I reasoned that it was better for Don to keep his mind busy, and we were thankful to Sandra and John for having this creative project for Don to do. Over the months from November to the end of February, Don lost fifty pounds.

We looked forward to our appointment on March 15 with Dr. Thompson for Don's physical, the ultrasound results would also be back by this time, and she would have had the opportunity to review Don's medical history. She would also consult her colleagues, including her husband, who in the months to come would play a huge part in Don's recovery. The days between appointments seemed long, and I read all I could on liver treatment. Our druggist has a great knowledge of vitamin therapy, and without his care, concern, and prayers I would have been unable to continue to help Don in this way as my knowledge was limited. Each day was filled with answered and unanswered questions.

I wondered -what could be causing the pain Don was now feeling in his stomach? Why was his stomach upset? My mind was working in circles. I can only imagine what was going on in Don's mind as I chased these questions 'round and 'round myself. We counted the days until the appointment for his physical on March 15.

At Don's physical the doctor ordered major blood work to inform herself of Don's current condition. Dr. Thompson had told Don's story to the nurses at the liver clinic. Dr Thompson told us at this point that though she was not a liver specialist, she knew that Don's liver was very diseased and he would need to see a specialist.

Our appointment with the liver clinic was booked, and the office called to set a date for Don to see a Hepatology specialist, that appointment was made for the morning of April 13, 2005, getting in that fast was a miracle. The month of April was the quietest month that we would have for several months; of course we did not know that at the time. Don kept busy with his patio work, even though his health was failing and fluid was gathering in his legs and abdominal cavity. All we could do was to wait for our appointment on April 13.

On two occasions I convinced Don to let me take him to the emergency room in our home town, hoping that they would be able to give him some relief. There was a resident doctor there who showed concern, and ordered more blood tests, which were also sent to Dr. Thompson, this gave me a feeling of comfort. They also ordered stronger diuretic pills for Don to see if we could slow down the fluid retention.

The morning of April 13th arrived, with great anticipation Don, his Dad, and I were in the car ready for the one and a half hour drive to the city. It is hard for me to describe my emotions. Certainly, happiness as we were going to see one of the top liver specialists. Thankfulness to Dr. Thompson who put this plan in place for us, and helped us get an appointment with this specialist. And, fear also crept into my mind, as I contemplated what the result of this visit would be. I could not even begin to imagine what Don must have been feeling, knowing that his body was once again failing. With the help of God and the Foothills medical team, we were ready to face the next part of this journey.

The first visit at the Hepatologist was comprised mostly of filling out forms, and answering questions. The first question was – when did you have your last drink?

Don answered, "August 20, 2004." then looked to me for confirmation.

More blood tests were done at that appointment. Every doctor we saw seemed to need their own set of blood work. No doubt, and rightfully so, they all checked for blood alcohol levels along with many other indicators that would be important in this next part of our journey. The afternoon visit with the liver specialist was in his private office, rather than at the liver clinic, as at this point, Don was not yet a patient of his. The first procedure here too, was a mass of forms to fill out and questions to answer. Twenty minutes later a doctor in his late 40's, sporting a brush cut and a turtle neck sweater came into the room. The tension in the room was broken with a simple handshake with Don, and I introduced myself. Dr. Meyer pulled his chair so that he could sit face to face with Don, their knees almost touching. His first words were, "When did you have your last drink?"

This became the question that Don would be asked first regardless of whom he saw, or who was caring for him, from doctors, to nurses, to lab technicians – absolutely everyone. As I think back answering questions was a struggle at this appointment because it was such a tense time as we were all fearful that the outcome would not be what we wished it to be. Dr. Meyer had a number of reports in his hand, the ultrasound and lots of blood tests. His voice was clear and firm as he briefly told Don about a couple of the tests. He could see by our faces, that we did not completely understand the meaning of the test results he was reading. What he would say next would emphasize to us the terrible seriousness of the situation.

He said to Don, "You have end stage liver disease, a disease for which there is no cure. At the stage you are now at, the only help for you would be a liver transplant. Without it you may have one and a half years to live."

How can I even try to put into words our feelings? In fact I can't even finish this sentence...

I silently prayed for strength for Don, his Dad, and I as we left the office building.

Over the next little while I came to realize that liver transplant is a treatment for liver disease, but it is not a cure. One will not be able to live a 'normal' life after the transplant, as one will have to take medication every day, have regular tests to ensure and check-up on the functioning of the transplanted liver, as well as regular doctor visits. A good life is possible; one just must pay attention to one's health. The Hepatologist decides if you meet the requirements, and then passes the information onto the assessment coordinator who will arrange and complete your assessment. Learning that you need a transplant is very stressful. It is mandatory that you have a support person throughout the whole process, for Don this was not a concern, as I was already in this position. There is so much information given to families about liver disease and the transplant process. The assessment will take up to six weeks to complete. Once it is complete, the decision will be made as to if you would be a good candidate for the transplant list. The waiting time for a liver is about one and a half years. Dr. Meyer had told Don that he would only have one and a half years without this treatment.

The assessment is an information gathering stage. The purpose is to help determine if a liver transplant is the best option for each patient, given their medical condition. With this information the journey began, to get Don on the list as soon as possible. We knew very well that time was not on our side. Appointments seemed too far away, and sometimes it was hard to remember that Don was not the only patient in this large geographic area. Despite what seemed like long breaks between appointments we understood. We kept eating well and using vitamins to help Don keep as strong as we could.

You are not accepted by the pre-op transplant team until all tests and information requested is received, and the whole team has a chance to meet and discuss your case. All persons with a history of alcohol abuse will be required to have an assessment by their provincial addictions counseling association, in Don's case AADAC. In addition to this they must be free of alcohol for six months. With all of these requirements to meet the endless appointments continued.

The first test to meet the transplant requirements was on April 14, 2005. It was a fasting blood test, and as such could not be done the day before when we were all ready in the city. The next two weeks were waiting times; Don was filling with fluid and becoming weaker. At the liver clinic we were assigned Alexis, as our coordinating assessment nurse, she would organize Don's tests. She was like having our very own guardian angel. We could phone her any time during the week to ask questions, or seek her advice, which we desperately needed. We also were told to call the Foothills Hospital to speak with the liver specialist on call if need be. We were so well cared for; it was comforting to have the 24 hour care and concern. This was a great relief to us as Don's health was rapidly deteriorating.

May 6, 2005 Don was back for more blood work. They were monitoring his liver function, or the lack there of. During this time of preparation Don would have to be available at the call of his cell phone to go for random blood tests to check for alcohol in his blood, if he did not go for these tests the team would assume that he had been drinking and this would seriously impact his assessment and placement on the transplant list.

As Don and I were traveling back and forth to the city we had a chance to visit and the bond between us and our trust for each other grew. We always managed to stop at our favorite cafe for lunch; this was a very special time for me. Having lunch with Don was something that I had never really done before. Already we were experiencing the wonderful moments that we had never before shared. May

11, 2005 was our next appointment at the early hour of 7:15 A.M. it was for an esophagus check at the hospital. The purpose of this procedure was to check for bleeding in the esophagus. Don was given a bed in a unit room where he was tested to see if he could undergo the test. This took most of our day, but we were patient, and very thankful to the nurses and wonderful caregivers who were there to help us. Often during this time I was reminded of a hymn that our friend, Pastor Art Dalen sang on a tape that he recorded, it was called *Thru It All*. "Thru it all, thru it all, Oh I've learned to trust in Jesus, I've learned to trust in God, I've learned to depend upon His Word."

May 16, we were back to Calgary for more follow up blood work. The tests had to be done there so that they could get immediate results. The assessment team needed ongoing information to track Don's fast changing health condition. On Wednesday May 18, 2005, we had another appointment with Dr. Thompson, at that time she called her husband, Dr. Scott in to consult with her in regards to the fluid that Don was retaining. Dr. Scott ordered another blood test to see if Don's blood was capable of clotting properly in order for him to drain the fluid without causing haemorrhaging. The test results showed that Don needed two injections of vitamin K to thicken his blood in preparation for this procedure. This meant that we needed to go back to the city the next day to get a vitamin K shot. On May 28, 2005, we had an appointment at the hospital where Dr. Scott worked, for another vitamin K shot and then the draining procedure. I guess if we were counting, that was 4 exhausting days that week, and the assessment process had only begun.

Don was now in the process of preparing for a transplant. During the past couple of months when Don was not strong enough to work on the patio he began to remodel his basement. He definitely had inner strength and had the willpower to push ahead. Despite the difficulties that this time brought to Don he never gave up, each day he amazed me with his determination and strength. I have heard other stories where the patient became cranky or disinterested in life. Don continued to be thankful for all of the help that was offered to him. My friends and I continued to pray.

May 31, 2005, we had a 10:00 A.M. appointment with Dr. Thompson. It was a check-up and more blood tests, so she could be updated on Don's condition. She explained how important it was for her to visually see Don, as well as the test results. We took so much comfort and encouragement from our visits with her that we looked forward to going. What a wonderful person she is, and was, to have been so caring and involved with us during this difficult time. Later that same day we had an appointment with Dr. Meyer at the liver clinic. At this time they outlined and explained what Don would be required to do in preparation for a transplant. The transplant team is a multi-disciplinary group made up of doctors, nurses, social workers, physiotherapists, occupational therapists, dieticians, and pastoral care personnel. They work together to determine the best course of action, based on the individual's circumstances. During the assessment process patients see all of the transplant team members all of whom showed concern and compassion for Don. They gave us hope.

The liver transplant surgery is performed at the University of Alberta Hospital, in Edmonton. The three life threatening symptoms of end-stage liver disease are:

1. Vomiting of blood or passing black stools
2. Mental confusion that leads to coma
3. Abnormal fluid build up in the abdomen that becomes infected.

Some of the other signs and symptoms include;

- Yellowing of eyes and skin
- Severe itching
- Dark tea colored urine
- Grey or clay colored stools
- Easy bruising and tendency to bleed
- Malnutrition
- Nausea
- Diarrhea
- Loss of muscle mass
- Muscle cramping
- Tendency to have osteoporosis
- Difficulty sleeping
- Fatigue
- Spider Veins around face, arms, and chest.
- Swollen ankles
- Pain in the area of the liver

We arrived home at the end of the day with all of this information to process in our minds. It was overwhelming.

We had been given a liver transplant pre-op teaching manual, this book never left my sight. By now I had collected many information sheets which I had organized into a large binder. After reading it over and over that evening, I added this new book to my growing collection. We had supper in the city on the evening of our appointments, and we dropped a very tired Don off at his home around 8:00 P.M. It was hard to leave him there, but somehow your own bed is the place that you most want to be after a day like this. Don had trouble sleeping, so his nights were long, and this new information would no doubt be swirling through his mind, as his body kept him awake. Once again my heart was broken as I closed the door, after he was settled into bed.

CHAPTER 7

What Would Today Bring?

*J*UNE 1, 2005, brought a morning filled with sunshine. I was thankful for a pretty good nights rest, and I busied myself with household chores, then sat at the island in my kitchen going over all of the symptoms we needed to watch for in our son, some of which I realized Don was all ready experiencing. I was bewildered by the number of concerns there were. Even though an end stage liver patient may have only a few symptoms, in the next months Don had all of them, and never just one at a time.

About 9:30 that morning I walked to the cupboard to warm my morning tea, when I saw a white pick-up truck drive up. I glanced out the window and realized that it was Don in his "new" pick-up. He had traded about a week ago. I guess it was something that my mind had no room to remember, because I was thinking of so many other things. Don always came over in the morning, so this was a normal thing, what happened next was not.

Don walked in and stood just inside the front door and said, "Mom, I don't feel right."

"Do you have any pain, or are you sick to your stomach?" I asked.

Don quickly and sharply replied, "I said, Mom I don't feel right."

Again my reply was, "I don't know what you mean?"

Don turned and said, "Oh never mind, I am going home."

I quickly followed him outside, and to my astonishment, Don did not know how to open his truck door. I said, "Well, Don it opens just like your other truck." This angered Don, much to my surprise.

I opened the door, and he got in, and I ran to the passenger side, and sat beside him in the truck. He did not know what to do with the keys or what they were, I said, "Let me have them, I'll show you." My mind was now racing back to the liver manual, and focusing on the term – mental confusion. This certainly must be what they meant I thought. I held the keys tightly in my hand and said, "Let's go back into the house Don." Don would not move. I realized then that Don did not know who he was, or where he was, nor did he know who I was. I ran to the phone to call his Dad and I dialed 9-1-1.

Both Don's Dad and I angered Don at this point. He was out of the truck and we could not go near him. The ambulance arrived quickly, and I told them that Don had end stage liver disease. The ambulance driver knew immediately what was going on, as he had been through the same type of reaction with his own father, as he had also suffered through end-stage liver disease.

The ambulance driver asked us to stand back, and reassured us that it was normal for patients in Don's situation to turn on those who were closest to them. It was about ten minutes before they could coax Don to the stretcher. How could this happen so fast I wondered? We followed the ambulance to the hospital, and hurried in. The doctor on call came. Our hospital is a small town hospital, the doctors are family physicians, not specialists. The doctor on call did not seem to grasp the seriousness of this condition, even though I had told them that Don had end stage liver disease. The little bit of information I had about confusion came from the post-operative manual which I had just read about one hour before this incident. The doctor asked if I could take Don home and stay with him. It was then that the ambulance driver spoke up and urged the doctor to get Don to the Foothills Hospital immediately. Don was unconscious and on a stretcher with the sides up. The doctor then asked if I could drive him there. This angered me, it seemed as though this was an experience that was unnecessary. The nurse then stepped in and things happened very fast after that and soon Don was on his way via ambulance.

Don's Dad and I stopped at home and quickly filled a suitcase with the essentials for a few days away, so we could be with our son. I quickly phoned our Pastor, Pat, even though he did not know Don, he was very much a part of my support network. He said he would stay by the phone, and would come when he heard from me if necessary. This was our first experience being in an emergency room at a large hospital. EMS and stretchers lined the halls in the emergency area. The waiting room was packed. In the triage unit they assess each individual and attend to them based on their medical needs, giving the quickest attention to those who need it most. Don was taken in immediately. When the paramedics transferred Don into a bed in a curtained area, he was completely oblivious to his surroundings. The doctors and nurses (at the Foothills Emergency Room) swarmed into the curtained room, it was unbelievable. Don's Dad and I stepped out when they began working on him. Tubes were inserted in his throat, and his nose, IV's, blood tests and monitors were started. We knew Don was where he would get the best help. We called our daughters and our other son. Both of Don's sisters arrived in less than two hours to support their brother, his brother remained at home as hospitals were uncomfortable for him, he reacted by continuing to work hard, no doubt with his brother in his thoughts. The confusion was caused by the failure of the liver to remove ammonia and other toxins from the blood stream. Laxatives such as lactulose must be given to help absorb toxins, and remove them from the system as soon as possible. The lactulose was given to Don through a tube inserted in his mouth. To a family, seeing our son and brother like this was disheartening, and frightening. I called Pastor Pat and he arrived at Don's bedside. We said a prayer, then Pastor Pat, Don's Dad, and I went to the cafeteria to have a cup of tea. Don's sisters stayed at his bedside. While we were gone, Don became coherent enough to recognize them for a moment.

Later that day Sandra and Kathy went home, and Don's Dad and I left the hospital to get a hotel room. We went back to the hospital and stayed there until midnight, when we were assured that Don was resting well enough for us to leave. This experience was the first of many that brought us to the Foothills Hospital Emergency. June 2, Don was moved to a room. In the afternoon one of the doctors was checking him and asking questions. This also had become part of the process in analyzing his condition. "Do you know where you are?" they would ask.

"No, I just know that I am not home." he would reply.

"Do you know where home is?"

"No, I just know that I am not home."

"Do you know your name?"

"No, not right now."

The doctor put his hand on my shoulder and said, "Do you know who this is?"

With a big smile Don said, "That's my Mom."

With that answer the doctor smiled and said, "Don, you're doing fine."

The specialist took this hospital stay as an opportunity to run some of the tests, that Don needed to get on the transplant list. They also drained four quarts of fluid from his abdomen. Don was released from the hospital on June 6. This time he was unable to return to his own home. His health was slipping fast, and the fear of another onset of confusion determined that Don would have to return to our home. We were fortunate to have a developed lower level, with an open stairway from our kitchen/ living room area. The room was furnished with two single beds, which after a short while, I pushed together making a king size bed for Don. I covered the beds with a King size topper to make it comfortable. We called it "the suite". We moved the television from the family room into Don's suite. He was very comfortable, and most importantly he was not alone. Don had to take the lactulose often during the day, and records of his bathroom visits had to be kept. Each day there were many decisions to be made, and we often phoned our liver coordinator. I fixed nutritious meals, some of which Don ate, and others which he did not quite feel up to eating. Don had to be tested for TB, Hepatitis, and have a dental appointment. All of these could be done in our hometown.

June 13, was the TB test, June 14 we drove to the city to meet with the AADAC center. We made another appointment for June 16, with the worker he would be assigned. June 17, brought us back to the city for an education session with the liver coordinator. June 19, we left for Edmonton, where the surgery would take place when the time was right. We had three solid days of appointments and tests at the University Of Alberta Hospital in preparation for the transplant. Don was tired and his memory was showing signs of confusion. We arrived home on the evening of June 22, once again exhausted from the experience. Monday June 27, we had another appointment with Doctor Thompson, for more blood work and other tests that the liver specialist required her to do, this was another seven hour day. The morning of June 28, Don came into the kitchen and was extremely confused. We got him in the car and were on our way to the Foothills Emergency Room once again. Once again triage got him in at once, and we spent the day at his bedside. He was released that evening.

Our trips to Calgary were always interesting and I learned a lot about the emergency medical department at the Foothills Hospital. Certainly we saw and heard about things that in our small town experience, we never even thought about. We were amazed at the quick wonderful care that was given. The patience that was shown for the drug addict in the next bed, the number of specialists and concerned professionals that visited his bedside, only to be rejected. The young girl across the narrow hall that had broken a needle in her arm while using drugs. The screaming and wailing that came from her lips as she curled up in the fetal position, and rejected the help that was there for her. The grandfather that had suffered a heart attack, and now lay surrounded by his loving family. The emergency room was there for anyone who needed their services. Seeing all of this makes me realize that we should pray daily for all of the caregivers who are there to help us through these bad times. For the Foothills Hospital I give thanks.

During the next six days we had no appointments in the city. Don had his dental check, and the required letter assessing his dental health was completed. Dental problems can be a source of infection after a liver transplant. A letter was also required for the transplant team in regards to the TB and Hepatitis tests. All vaccinations are also required to be up to date, as well as vaccinations for Hepatitis A and B before the transplant takes place.

It seemed that Don was either freezing or too hot, and in the evenings he suffered from muscle cramps. Don was weak and very thin by now. I would rub his legs, feet, and hands many times during the day and night. We would alternate between hot and cool rubs, none of them doing the job. Don would say, "Mom rub harder, I can't feel it." My hands would be rubbing with all of my strength, but this was nothing compared with the cramps. Don could not take anything orally to help, as his body could not process the medication. This nightly ritual went on for the next three months.

July 5, 2005, Don was booked at the Rockyview Hospital with the lung specialist,

Doctor Scott took an x-ray of his lungs, and then more fluid was drained. The fluid was always tested for infection, Don on many occasions had to be given IV's to treat the infections that were detected in the draining process.

On July 8, 2005, we had another appointment with Doctor Meyers, at these appointments Don would see each member of the transplant team, it would take two hours in total. Don was put on numerous medications at this appointment, to try to keep him healthy and his liver functioning, at the level it was. The social worker, one of the team members, was there to help provide emotional support, and financial counseling if needed. Don was fortunate to have his mortgage insured and two other insurance policies. One covered hospitalization, and the other disability. These policies eased the burdens that a person suffering from ill health encounters. Someone needing a liver transplant because of alcohol abuse is required to go into a treatment centre for twenty-one days. Due to the fact that Don's health was failing so quickly, and that he needed so much care, the transplant team agreed that he could attend the Daily Intensive Treatment Centre for ten days, this program was offered at an ADDAC centre in Calgary. The sessions started on July 18th, this was ten days that none of us will forget. Our alarm rang at six o'clock and we needed to be out of the house and on the road by seven o'clock, as our destination was downtown Calgary and we needed to arrive there with the regular rush hour traffic. Don was on strong diuretics at this time, so we needed to allow for stops along the way. When we arrived at the centre, my heart ached for my son. It reminded me of when Don was in the sixth grade, and we had just arrived in our new home town. I remember watching as my son walked towards the school door and slowly opened it, not knowing what was to come next. I could still see that little boy in the shadow of my full grown son, and my heart ached knowing there was nothing that I could do to comfort or prepare him for what was to come. He would just have to get through it.

The sessions started at 9:00 a.m. and there was a short break mid-morning, and mid-afternoon, and lunch at noon, the day would end at four o'clock. As Don left the vehicle that morning his Dad and I looked at each other, and the reality of our situation hit us. Here we were with seven hours of the day to fill, in a city away from home. We could not leave the street as Don was in no condition to be left on his own, our solution was to walk up and down the street. We shopped and browsed aimlessly at the few stores in the area. Not being a shopper one trip in each store was enough for me. Luckily there was a large Co-op store across the street from the ADDAC centre, it had a great deli and a nice spot to eat in upstairs, the bathrooms were nice too. After the second day of 'loitering' I spoke with the store manager and told him about our situation, so he would not think we were there to cause problems. He welcomed us and told us to make ourselves at home. Throughout this journey we encountered angels everywhere. The eating area had tables and chairs, as well as large leather chairs, books to read, and was just generally a pleasant place to be. Don's Dad had just finished his latest construction project, and at this time knew that I needed his help with all that was happening. His crew found other work and he was free to be with Don and I, to help with all of the traveling and appointments. This was quite a change for my husband, sitting in large comfortable chairs was not how he was used to spending his days, however he was glad for the opportunity to be with us, and it was important that he was there to help.

Don came out to our car during his breaks, to see us and he was thankful for the break from the intensity of the class. The third day when Don came to the car at his morning break he was extremely upset. Usually Don was not too much for talking in his sessions, but this morning he realized that he needed to tell the others, young, and old what it was like to have the doctor tell him that he would only be alive, likely, for one and a half years longer. Three months of that one and a half years had all ready passed. He told them the emotions that they were talking about, such as having an argument with a girlfriend, did not even touch the emotions one experienced when they are told their days are numbered. He also expressed his embarrassment at having his seventy year old parents waiting in front of the centre, as if he were a little boy in grade school. He then stressed to the other participants how important it was to think about their choices before it was too late for them.

A few days later I was speaking to the instructor, who told me how well Don was doing in the class, and the impact that he was having on others. We counted down each day; some days we would stop for supper in the city, others Don would just get in the car and lie down in the back seat, and hardly make it into the house when we got home. I tried some evenings to put something in the slow cooker, so that we could have something good to eat when we got home. We had no excuses not to have food, as we were spending most of our day in the Co-op grocery store.

As I think back I realize what an endurance test this was for all of us. We had a set goal and this was just another step up the mountain to save our son, we could and would do it.

On the eighth day of classes at ADDAC Don had an afternoon appointment with Doctor Meyers. This meant that rather than being in classes at ADDAC he would be spending two hours meeting with members of the transplant team. Don was weak and filling with fluid, an appointment was made for the next afternoon to have the fluid drained. The next morning at class was dreadful for Don, but he stayed in class, he labored to breathe, and did not feel well. We waited anxiously outside the centre, in the car in case an emergency arose.

That afternoon we went to the Rockyview Hospital and the nurses prepared Don for the draining of the fluid, this included a blood test, and waiting for results, then Doctor Scott began the process of draining once again. After an hour the draining was completed, but Don lost consciousness, this resulted in quick action at his bedside. Once again we wondered how much longer his body could fight to keep going. The doctor expressed his concern at Don being in this dangerous condition and still attending classes at the centre. We realized that the transplant team had a set of procedures that patients must follow, and that these classes were the final requirement that Don had to meet. Friday July 29th was the final day of the program at the ADDAC centre, Don had a very uncomfortable night the evening before. The alarm did not even need to ring. My husband and I awoke early, anxious to get this last day in. I went to Don's room and said "Okay Don, this is it, our last day."

"I am unable to go today Mom, I am too weak." he whispered.

"We are leaving in half an hour, so come on," Don's Dad said.

"Dad, you would have me go even if it kills me."

"It's our only chance to save you, and we are going." My husband replied

Without any further hesitation we were on our way to the city once again. Confusion was noticeable in Don's mental state as we arrived at the centre. I encouraged Don by saying, "Don, just go up to the class, we will be right here if you need us."

I went to the ADDAC office area a number of times that morning. It seemed almost cruel that Don had to be in the last hours of this class in such a weakened and confused state. At 12:30 Don came out of the building with his certificate of recognition stating that he had successfully completed the Intensive Day Treatment Program. I prayed that this single blue piece of paper would be the lifeline that would save my son's life.

On July 30th, Don was still struggling with confusion but by that evening Don was resting more comfortably and the confusion was lessening. By this time I had set up a baby monitor between my room and Don's, with this I could hear his breathing, and therefore could get to his room before he needed to call me. The monitor was a great relief for me. Monday to Thursday of that week, Don continued to lose strength. Friday morning I called the liver specialist at the Foothills Hospital, he arranged for us to go to High River to have blood work done, and then assured us that he would get the results from that test immediately. We waited at the hospital for the results; from here we found out that Don's potassium levels were high, and his sodium levels were low. Don had been on a low sodium diet; the doctor changed his diet slightly and took him off of the diuretic pills. We returned for another blood test on Sunday, which showed improvement.

In life we are fortunate to have one friend who remains a friend from school days through adulthood. Don has such a friend. Kevin has spent most of his adult life in Fort McMurray. In his younger years after both he and Don had finished school they worked together in various construction jobs. When Kevin married he moved to Fort McMurray, and has had a very successful career with Suncor. Over the years they have talked on the phone regularly and visited each other when they could. When Don became ill Kevin's uplifting phone calls came even more regularly. Don would say to me, "Well, I got my motivational call from Kevin at six o'clock this morning, I should be good for another couple of days."

Kevin and Angie had been in touch with Don and were taking all of their family, including their grandchildren to Drumheller, for a holiday and to visit the dinosaur museum. Kevin wanted Don to come to visit them. Even though Don was weak, we decided that he would rest in the back seat of the car, and we would drive him the two- and a half hours to spend the evening with Kevin and his family. This would be good therapy for Don. After we had a nice supper, Don and Kevin spent the evening visiting in Don's hotel room. Kevin has a loud hardy laugh, and I am sure that there was a lot of reminiscing and laughter that evening. The next morning Kevin had arranged for a room at Smitty's where we all met for breakfast. Getting to know Kevin's kids and grandchildren was so much fun. After breakfast we began our journey home, Don climbed in the back seat of the car and fell into an exhausted sleep. He was content and felt happy after this special time with his friend. My husband and I were also feeling the warmth of their friendship.

During the previous few days Don had gained ten pounds of fluid. We had an eight o'clock appointment on August 10th for another draining procedure. He settled into a bed at the Foothills Hospital for the day as he had blood tests, was given blood plasma, and albumin, had an ultrasound, and the fluid drained. Another full day of special care. We still had not received any information to inform us that Don had been accepted onto the transplant list.

August 12 to 16th 2005, Don's breathing was extremely labored. Early on the morning of the 16th the ambulance was called, and we were once again in the Foothills Emergency Room. There he was given more blood plasma, two pints of blood, had three liters of fluid drained, and an endoscopy. I stood by his bedside, wondering once again how long Don could keep body and soul together. Don was released on August 18th from this round of treatment.

August 19th we were back in the ambulance again returning to the Foothills Hospital. Don had filled with fluid so fast that he needed oxygen, and could no longer breathe on his own. It sounded like he was drowning in his own fluid. He was kept in emergency overnight, and late in the afternoon of August 20th they had a bed for him in the transplant unit. That evening Don's Dad and I went home relieved, knowing that Don was receiving excellent care. During that time they were trying to get Don stabilized. While in the hospital the internal medicine, lung and liver specialists were caring for him. Blood work was done regularly, in addition to a CAT scan, ultrasound, colonoscopy, and fluid was drained four times in the eleven days. The Foothills hospital is a training hospital, as such a couple of his drains were not quite as slick as he was used to. Don would say- "well they have to train, so I may as well help them along." He was released from this hospital stay on August 31.

Once again the special care of the Foothills Hospital exceeded anything that I had ever experienced. Doctors and nurses were extremely busy everywhere, helping not only to care for Don and their other patients, but also taking time to inform Don's Dad and I as to what was going on and Don's condition. Don was in the Foothills Hospital for over seventy days from June to September 2005. His experience and care could not have been better. For those of us outside of the medical and care giving occupations this experience was amazing, we were in wonder of how these wonderful people could give so much of themselves to each of their many patients. We always looked forward to going with Don to his appointments at the liver clinic, here too the staff offered their time, patience, encouragement, and warm care to all.

On August 22, 2005 we received a letter from Transplant Services at the University of Alberta Hospital confirming that Don was now listed as a liver transplant candidate. In the letter they stated that he must continue to see his referring physician every three months, and have monthly blood work done while waiting for a transplant. This pretty well told us that not every transplant patient endures the months of suffering that Don did. We realized that these months would give Don a second chance of life, and we were thankful for that.

People are placed on the transplant list according to three criteria;

    1. Blood Group

    2. Donor Weight and Size

    3. Status – this means how sick they are.

There are four separate liver transplant lists, one for each of the four blood types. The surgeons will determine the weight range of acceptable donors for each patient. This is so they can match the size of the liver to the recipient body. At the time of listing each patient is assigned a status based on their medical situation. If you are not in the hospital you will be the same status as all other recipients, if you are admitted to hospital the transplant team is notified and your status may change based on your medical needs at the time. People who are urgently ill will be transplanted before others on the list, no matter how long you have been on the list. Once you are on the transplant list you have a lot of planning to do. If you do not live in the same city as where the transplant will take place, or the close surrounding area, you must have plans made for yourself and a support person to stay in the city for two months after the transplant is done. You are reminded to get someone to manage your personal affairs such as monthly payments, watering the plants, and taking care of any other regular responsibilities. Don was fortunate as his sisters were able to help in all of these areas. Even in the months before Don was placed on the transplant list I was making preparations to be away. I had a suitcase packed to meet our needs for three days, and a large plastic container with a tight lid filled with items such as shampoo, laundry soap, my tea, and everything that I thought I would need for a two month stay. The three day suitcase was in the car from June on. I tied purple ribbons around the hangers of the clothes in the closet that my daughters were to bring to us when the transplant took place. The blue plastic container containing all of my essentials sat ready to be transferred to their car when we called. I even had a large supply of my 'health food' cookies baked and in the deep freezer. Kathy was given signing authority at the bank over our accounts so that she could take care of the bills. I wanted to make sure that our every thought went to Don's surgery and recovery. Buying toothpaste was not going to be a priority.

September 1, 2005, was our Fifty-fourth wedding anniversary, the day was uneventful in that regards. Don felt pretty good so we had a quiet, relaxing day at home. The next day Don was tired, and the day after that he slept all day which was unusual. There were times when Don was entering the condition of encephalopathy (confusion) he would call, "Mom. Mom." I would hear him over the monitor. I would rush to his bedside and give him more lactulose hoping that later he would make a trip to the bathroom. He needed encouragement and love. There was no shortage of this for my son. It really was Don and I that depended on each other. I was his support and he was mine. He gave all he could of himself to help me stay strong. He would say; Mom go have a rest, or Mom you better eat more supper. We were a team. I would not change anything that we struggled through together. There must be a saying about when hard times come it makes you stronger, if not I will just say, Don and I grew strong together. After I got him settled down I would creep back to my own bed. If the confusion was increasing he would not call 'Mom', instead he would call 'hello, hello, hello' there was fear in his voice, as it showed that he did not know where he was and needed help quickly. We knew he was not doing well when we heard this. Sometimes our reasoning was that we were just at the hospital, we can't call the ambulance again. We made decisions to go to the hospital more difficult than it should have been on this and other occasions. By five-thirty on the morning of September 5th we knew that we had waited too long. Don had quickly worsened and was not coherent, and was unable to walk. We dressed him with difficulty, by this time he was not able to help himself at all. These bouts of confusion could happen at any time. Our days at home were filled with ensuring that we met the strict diet schedule that was set out for Don. Taking lactulose, a variety of pills and vitamins, calling the liver coordinators to confirm about how much of this or that he should have, or if there was something else that I should be doing. Daily care changed based on the blood tests which were done every couple of days. The decisions were not daily, they were hourly. We were unable to leave Don alone, as he too also feared the daily unknown. We kept the pre-op liver book on the island in the kitchen, and it was always open and I knew it by heart. My regular life stopped on August 20, 2004 when Don told me he was ready to make a change. Just spending time with Don was important to both of our well being.

CHAPTER 8

Ongoing Care

We have an elevator going from the lower level of our home to the main floor, without this we would have had to call the ambulance, in hind-sight this is what we should have done anyway. After struggling to get Don into the car we raced to the Foothills Emergency Room. We went into the emergency room and got a wheelchair and asked for assistance, not knowing that the staff could not help outside of the hospital. We desperately needed some help, and a security guard came quickly to our aid. A nurse was waiting for us at the door and rushed Don through triage. We in turn received a bit of a scolding for not calling the ambulance.

She said, "I know you are going to say that you just used the ambulance and that you didn't think you could call again, but you could have."

We did get him there in ambulance time, it was a fast

ride, and no officer could catch up to us, I am sure. The fact that we made it still didn't make our choice right.

Once again as had happened many times before, tubes were inserted down Don's throat, through his nose and mouth, monitors and IV's were quickly attached and specialists were surrounding our son as they tried to stabilize him. This hospital stay lasted until September 8. On September 9th we had to be back at Rockyview Hospital where Doctor Scott would again drain the fluid, this time three liters of fluid was drained from Don's abdominal cavity. Don's blood pressure dropped therefore most of the day was spent at the hospital. They brought Don a small lunch, and after his blood pressure was normalized we were back in the car headed home.

The past months there had been many nights where I spent many hours with Don in his room. When I became tired I would lay down beside him as I would when he was a little boy long ago, reaching my hand out to comfort his hurts and reassure him I was still there. I even hummed the same lullabies that I had once hummed to sleeping babies many years earlier. I was back taking care of my little boy again, and this time it seemed so much harder. Don's desire to survive was so strong, he never quit fighting to grasp onto any thread of life that was there for him to cling to. Sometimes when wanting to pray it was hard to know what to say to God. First I thanked Him for all of our blessings, and for all of the special people we had come in contact with. When you are on the transplant list you suddenly realize that someone must die for you to live. Don struggled with this. It was as though we were truly understanding the sacrifice that our Lord had made for us as He allowed His only son to be sacrificed on the cross, for our life.

As I prayed for my son to be the recipient of a liver, I needed help from our Pastor Pat as to how best deal with the prayer I was seeking. After all in order for my prayer to be answered someone else's prayers would likely have to be denied. On one occasion our pastor went to visit Don, as Don slept he sat quietly in his room praying for him. When Don awoke Pastor Pat spoke to Don about the donor and their family. Don felt more comfortable after this conversation. I knew there were many friends praying for Don and our family as we went through this remarkable experience.

September 13 brought another appointment with the lung specialist where more chest X-ray's of the lungs were done, and more fluid drained. On September 16 we were back in the city for an appointment with the psychologist, as our liver coordinator was concerned about how Don was dealing with the stress of the appointments and the conflicting thoughts about the upcoming transplant, what it would mean for him, but also what it would cost others. Don was not pleased about this appointment, but he went anyways, just as he always did, to do whatever was necessary to save his life. This was one time he said he would go if it made me feel better. It did.

September 17 and 18th 2005, Don could hardly breathe. On the 19th we were back at the lung specialist for an unscheduled appointment in an effort to help relieve Don's breathing. Three more liters of fluid was drained, and again Don fainted, even though I had made sure that he had something to eat before the procedure. At this point Don's appetite was flagging, we were using a protein drink and trying to find foods that would appeal to him and meet the demands dictated by his diet. September 20th Don was understandably very tired. He felt wobbly and shaky – this sent us back to the Foothills Hospital, as these were symptoms we had not seen before. The lung specialist had recommended that the next time Don was admitted to hospital that he should be kept there until he received a transplant. This time Don stayed.

We had read that many patients were hospitalized for sometime before their transplant. We had prepared ourselves for this and Don did not want to come home. The traveling back and forth and the uncertainty of his condition was getting to be a large burden to bear, regardless we knew that God never gives us more than we can handle, and we were prepared to continue forward as long as necessary. This stressful time required more than just my simple lullabies. During the next week Don went through more testing, more draining, more fainting, more confusion, all of this between visits with his concerned family. Don's Dad and I spent most of everyday with him, in his room and wandering around the hospital, eating in the cafeteria, and then back to Don's room. The care for him was continual. When I hear people complain about hospital services, I don't understand it, we saw and experienced nothing but the best and most conscientious care offered to all patients.

We stayed in touch with Kevin, and he talked with Don often, and knew all that was taking place. Sodium, ammonia, and blood pressure were just some of the problems that the medical team were dealing with. We trusted completely in the decisions that they made. On October 5, 2005, things were going along the same as they had been all week. Don's Dad and I got home in the early evening, and planned to return to the hospital after lunch the next day. At 8A.M. on October 6, the phone rang, it was the hospital, Don had gone into a coma. They did not have any answers yet, but he had been taken to intensive care. We phoned our family, and left for the city, not knowing what our next challenge would be.

Don was still in a coma, his sisters arrived quickly. We took turns being in his room, and waiting outside the door. The specialists were making decisions, and later plans to air lift our son to the University Hospital in Edmonton. My heart was heavy as I watched my son lay quietly in a coma.

Dear, God, I prayed thank-you for being with Don. Give him the strength that he needs to recover from this trauma. Prayer was ongoing on my lips, and in my heart. Kevin was called immediately, we would notify him if and when, Don was moved. About seven o'clock in the evening the nurses told us that they were making plans for Don to be moved. They explained the procedure that would be followed to transport Don to Edmonton. They knew he would be leaving sometime during the night, but did not have an exact time. Don was stable, but still in a coma. My husband, and I went to check into a hotel for the evening, and then out to supper with our daughters. At 8:00 P.M. our cell phone rang. It was the hospital, they would be moving Don in one hour. It became necessary to get him to Edmonton as quickly as possible. After a quick discussion Kathy and Sandra went back to the hospital to be with Don as he left by air ambulance. We quickly checked out of the hotel, and were on our way to Edmonton to the University hospital. As I try to explain how I felt at this time, I am not sure I can. I guess the best way to describe it is that I was just in the moment, I was focused on what was happening right now, processing what was happening and how I would respond. I thought only of Don and getting to the hospital at this time. I was thankful that we were there, thankful that Kathy and Sandra would be at the hospital to be with Don as he left. Even though he was in a coma, they spoke to him, and reassured him that we would be waiting for him in Edmonton, reassuring him that he was loved, and praying that things would be okay.

As we left Calgary we called our other son Ken, there was quiet on his end of the phone, and he quietly said he would call us back. Our next call was to Kevin. It was then that I got a little pep talk, Kevin had been on the internet, when Don had first become sick and was very knowledgeable about the process of liver disease and transplant. That made it easier for him to speak with us with great authority, assuring us that this was a good thing. If Don was at the hospital, he would have the transplant sooner. Once again the concerns, and care for the donor family was heavy on my heart. We realized of course that a transplant would not be immediate, some people wait in hospital for any given length of time. The weather was so good on October 6, 2005, that the drive was relatively easy. Phone calls were being placed and received as we made our way to Edmonton. Don's Dad and I spoke only occasionally, to reassure each other that everything was going to go well. Most of the trip was made in silence, except for the sharp ring of the phone.

Kevin called as we traveled making sure that we were driving safely, and letting us know that he and his wife would be there on Sunday. Another call came in from Don's brother, unable to hold back tears as he spoke. We assured him that it was a good thing that Don was going to the Edmonton hospital, and that things were going to be okay. I am sure that the phone calls in the dark of the night made the drive go quickly. The loving concern for Don and my husband and I was a comfort during this dark drive to the unknown.

CHAPTER 9

The Gift of Life

As we had been to Edmonton on the previous trips in preparation of the transplant we had found the quickest and easiest route to the hospital, a place to park, and the door that was nearest to where we needed to be. Now all of this information was appreciated as we arrived in the city at 11:30 P.M.. We left our three-day suitcase in the vehicle, as we did not know where we would be staying, or if we would even leave the hospital. We quickly found the intensive care unit. The nurses were anxious to help us, they took us to a small family room where we could wait until we could see Don. A social worker came to see us to make sure we knew what was happening, and to give us directions to the Out Patient Residence, where we could stay for a few nights. We were given a pass for parking, had our coats hung up, and offered coffee. The concern for us was wonderful. It was about one hour before we could see Don. Because Don was brought in from another hospital, the nurses and anyone going into the ICU had to have gowns, masks, and gloves on. This preventative measure was taken to ensure that no infections were transferred from one hospital to another. Don was still in a coma. He was attached to machines, monitors and IV's, he also had a breathing machine. I cannot describe all that was taking place because I am a Mom, not a medical person. It was overwhelming to see my Son surrounded by all of this equipment. It was a miracle that he was being kept alive, thanks to the modern technology.

I spoke to Don, even though he seemed unaware that we were even there. His Dad could not hold back tears as he touched his covered legs and feet. I seemed to have an amazing amount of strength as we stood and watched. The doctors left the room, and two nurses, one on each side took over the monitoring. My strength came from my strong belief in God, I knew we were not alone, I could feel His presence, as I put my trust and faith in Him. About two o'clock in the morning the social worker returned, she was concerned about us. The nurse suggested that we go to our room, and assured us that they would call if there was any change. I prayed silently for my Son as I turned and left the intensive care unit.

The walk to the room had many turns, luckily there were arrows to direct us there, it must have taken ten minutes, the hospital was connected to the residence, so we did not even have to go outside. When we finally arrived in the room, my husband had to try to figure out where the parking lot was so he could go retrieve our suitcase. We had turned so many corners, I wondered if we would ever get it straightened out. The room was tiny, maybe even very tiny. The beds were old hospital beds, I think, but did they ever look good to us – it had been a long day. Early the next morning we found our way to the cafeteria and had a small breakfast then quickly returned to the intensive care unit. Don was still in a coma, but was beginning to be a little more restless. Could this mean he was coming out of the coma I wondered? Shortly after we arrived Don's eyes opened and we were able to speak with him. Words cannot express the joy we felt. Don had a breathing tube which assisted him with his breathing, this tube was attached to a ventilator, because of this he was not able to speak. He was awake and knew we were there. The nurses were talking to him explaining where he was and how he got there. He was responding to the treatment slowly. The doctors arrived and felt that he was doing as well as he could, he was still very sick, his kidneys, his lungs, and his liver were all being monitored. We knew our Son had care that could not be surpassed.

I was amazed to find that as we met new people in many different places, the number of them who had also been touched through their families by alcoholism. I was able to share pieces of Don's story, hoping to provide encouragement to these people and their families, to let them know that it could be beat.

Later in the day Don's Dad and I set out to find a place to stay for the next two months. There was an apartment building across the street where apartments could be rented by the month, but they were full. We wanted a place near the hospital. The clinic had given us a list of places to call, and we checked them all. It was somewhat hard for we needed two bedrooms and two baths, as we needed a place for Don after he was released from his surgery. We found a couple of places that were not too clean, or were filled with smoke. When we arrived back at the hospital I went back over the list crossing off those we did not want, finally the list had a line through every name.

Don was resting as comfortably as could be expected, he still had a breathing tube, and thus could not speak. Outfitted in our gowns and masks we told him about the phone calls from home, and our search for our home away from home. We did not stay in the room very long at a time, but we came often. We stayed at the hospital all day. The cafeteria had good meals, and the people in the waiting rooms were all friendly. When you are in an ICU waiting room there are many sad stories, but there are also many great stories with wonderful outcomes. We spent the night in the tiny room at the hospital, we were very thankful for that service.

The morning of October 8, 2005, my husband and I moved into the Best Western Hotel, only six minutes from the hospital. Our room had an adjoining room, and the hotel went out of their way to accommodate us. They would rent Donnie's room next door, and then as soon as we knew that he was going to be out we were to let them know so they could make sure that the room was available. The hotel had a nice cafe, and our room had a table, a couple of comfy chairs, and a refrigerator. This was the best solution for us. My sister Helen and her husband Wes lived in Fort Saskatchewan, only forty-five minutes away, this allowed us to be served several delicious home cooked meals at their lovely home, giving us a real break from the hospital. This was even more special as this was the first time my sister and I really has opportunity to be together, as we have a significant age difference, and we did not live near each other.

There was a Super Store across the street from the hotel, to meet any of our needs. We settled in expecting the big suitcases and plastic container on October 9th when Kathy and Sandra arrived. The two month plan was working well.

As this was a new experience for us, we were shocked to learn that Don was not on the transplant list at this time. When it was explained to us it made sense. He could not undergo surgery in the condition that he was in. Now the improvement in Don's health was even more urgent, he needed to be well enough for a transplant. As the doctors watched his numbers from blood work, they would comment on them – this is a little better this morning, but something else would be the same. They continued to work with Don to get him healthy enough to be put back on the list. Sunday, October 9th, was exciting as Kathy and Sandra were arriving and bringing all of the things that we would need, or at least I thought I needed for our stay. Anyway, I will say I was well prepared.

After they arrived we had a light lunch and then returned to the hospital. When we rang the buzzer to announce ourselves to enter the ICU, we were told that Don already had company – so would we just stay a few minutes. We knew in a moment that Kevin and Angie were there. We walked in and there was Kevin, a big man, tall and sturdy, all gowned and masked and Don was getting his motivational talk. What a friend. He was such an important part of Don's recovery. On October 10th, Kevin and Angie were on their way home, and Don was moved to a bed outside the ICU. The next day he was moved to the liver unit. I joked with Don that we were getting closer but he was still not back on the transplant list. They now had a draining tube constantly secured into his abdominal cavity so he would not fill up again.

October 12th, Don was feeling a little better, he ate some lunch, and we were thrilled to hear that he had been put back on the transplant list. At this time Don was fighting to hang onto life with every breath he took, again I was amazed at the strength that Don was able to summon from his inner self. This was a very special time for us. At two o'clock that afternoon I went to get my hair done. My sister Helen and her husband Wes were coming in the afternoon. They would visit then we would all go out for supper. I am excited to report that our supper plans were changed – when at 5 P.M. a nurse came into the room, she said, "Hello Don, have you had anything to eat since lunch?"

"No," Don replied.

"Have you had anything to drink?"

I stood there, a shiver crept over my body, I knew what the next words would be. She pointed her finger at Don and said, "We have a liver for you."

Don rested his head back on the pillow and closed his eyes momentarily. Tears flowed down my cheeks, they flowed down my sisters cheeks, and no one spoke for minutes. Don had just been moved from intensive care and now his body would have to endure at least six hours of surgery. It would be opened, his organs moved to allow the diseased liver to be removed, and replaced with the precious gift of life he had been given.

Then my sister, who volunteers with victims services, seemed to have some words to say to Don at this time.

She broke the silence with, "This is what you're here for Don, so now is the time."

The nurses gave us a few minutes, then the attack on Don began. We were chased out and they brought in more machines, set up IV's, and bathed him. It was like a bee hive in the room for the next few hours. I would step in once in a while to make sure that Don knew that we were still there. When we got seated in the waiting room, Don's cell phone rang. It was Kevin, it was like he had a premonition. We told him they were preparing Don for surgery. I took the phone into Don.

"Mom, I can't talk to Kevin right now, I am too emotional," Don said.

Kevin understood, and I assured him we would call him soon. Don's Dad made phone calls to all of our family, talking with each one of them. As I sat in the waiting room outside Don's door I gave God all of the glory for allowing this to happen. I also prayed and cried for the family who had lost their loved one, so that my Son could have this most amazing gift.

This liver would be a cadeveric (brain dead) transplant, the family of someone who had died had given their loved ones organs as a gift of life. We are so thankful that even in their time of sadness and tragic loss, this family thought to give the gift of life by providing for organ donation, this time it saved my Son.

About 8:30 P.M. the bustle in Don's room slowed, we were able to go back in the room, until they needed to do another round of preparation. At one point I slipped into Don's room, he sat with his legs over the side of the bed, and again I wondered what the right words would be to offer to my Son at a time like this. I did not know. I took his hand and said, "Don

I know that this will be all right. I know because there are so many people praying for you."

"Mom, of course it will be good," Don said.

"I love you," I said, and then could not say any more.

A nurse came in and the silence was broken. The next time we noticed Don alone in the room his Dad took the cell phone in and dialed Kevin's number.

"Hi, Kevin, here is Don."

Don's hands shook as he reached for the phone, and his Dad left the room. Later Don told me some of that conversation.

Kevin said, "Don, I have been doing something that I haven't done in years. I have been praying for you. And my Mom has everyone in Prince Edward Island praying for you, and when Ann Demas prays things happen."

Don's reply was, "You know, Kevin, I have been praying too."

After they had finished talking Don lay back on the bed looking very peaceful and prepared to tackle the next chapter in his book of life. We visited with Don and I was thankful that Helen and Wes were with us. Helen was able to keep things going at a time that would have otherwise been even more difficult for my husband and I. At one point Don asked the nurse what some of the IV's were. The nurse told him that one was an antibiotic, another was an anti-viral and an anti-inflammatory, then Don piped up and said, "And there is my 'auntie' Helen." This brought a laugh from all of us.

Yes, we were ready for this, still shocked, and unable to believe that this was taking place only hours after Don's name was returned to the transplant list.

At 10:30 P.M. the nurse and the porters came to wheel Don into surgery. I will never forget that moment. Don looked straight ahead, raising his arm in a slight wave as he went by. We watched them disappear down the hall, we were all quiet. In a few minutes, my sister was giving me orders.

"You go back to your room and go to bed."

"I want to stay at the hospital," I replied.

"And what are you going to do? Help with the surgery?"

"No, I'll just be here," I said.

"You'll also be here in six minutes if they need you. Get your rest, you will need it," my sister said.

With that I agreed to go back to the room. If all went well the surgery would take about six hours. Don's Dad and I would return about 4:30 A.M.. I was to phone my sister in the early morning, after we returned to the hospital.

CHAPTER 10

The Perfect Match

WHEN YOU are taken to the operating room for a liver transplant this is what happens. The anaesthetist will ask a few questions, and then administer the aesthetic. After you are asleep the following tubes will be inserted:

- IV lines – to give fluids, salts, sugar, and medication.
- Central lines – these lines measure the volume of fluids in your body.
- Arterial lines – these lines measure your blood pressure.
- Endotracheal tube – this assists with breathing and is attached to a machine.
- Nasogastric tube – this tube drains the contents of your stomach.

- Foley Catheter – this drains the urine from the bladder.

Following surgery you may also have some additional tubes:

- Bile Tube – this tube drains bile and is used to x-ray your bile ducts, these drain the bile from your liver.
- Jackson Pratt Drains – these drain blood and body fluid from around the surgical area, you may have two or more of these tubes.

Don had all of the above.

During the operation the surgeon will remove your diseased liver, and reattach the new liver at five sites. Four of the sites are blood vessels, the fifth drains bile from the liver. Staples will hold the incision together. The incision is made down the front of the chest and from side to side under the ribs. A large bandage covers the incision. One of the draining tubes was placed under Don's right arm on the side of the chest.

We arrived back at the hotel, and I did as my sister told me. I got undressed and into bed to rest. The fact that Don was in surgery, and that there was a liver available for him at this time was yet another reason to give thanks for all that we had received. I prayed for Don, the medical team, and the donor family. At 4:30 on October 13, 2005, we were getting prepared to go back to the hospital. What a different feeling this was, compared to all of the times before. I felt relief, excitement, and joy for our son, and sorrow for the donor family.

Many times in a Mother's life it seems as though the logic of our hearts has more than one emotion to process at a time. Moments of happiness and sorrow. Don was not back in his room when we arrived. To our surprise the nurses told us that his sisters had just left. They had arrived at 4 A.M., bless their hearts, when they got the news that Don was in surgery, they decided to start driving, as sleep would surely not come to them. So they picked up extra-large Tim Horton's coffee and set off to be with their brother and us. Don was back in the ICU room at 6 A.M.. Certainly every tube that they had mentioned and told us about was in Don's body. Monitors were flashing and nurses, again, two, on each side were watching. Doctors were busy with their instructions. As Don's Dad and I stood silently in one spot, so as not to interfere with their work, a doctor said, "This went very well. The liver was a perfect match, that made it easier, he is doing very well."

I asked the coordinator what she could tell me about the donor, she said absolutely nothing. This is a very anonymous procedure.

Sandra and Kathy arrived back at the hospital about eight in the morning after a couple hours rest. They were anxious to look in on their brother, just to let him know that they were there. We were not sure how much of this Don absorbed, but it sure made us feel good.

On October 14th, Don had great vital signs and the doctor was very pleased. Don could not speak because of the breathing tube. The next time we went into Don's room, things had changed slightly. They had found a bacteria in the room Don was moved from, so we were back to isolation until they made sure that this infection had not entered Don's system. He was kept in isolation for three days, when they found that he did not have the infection. The breathing tube had been removed on the second day, allowing Don to talk some, but his throat was still very sore. All but one tube had been removed by October 16.

Kevin arrived on October 16th to "check things out". This gave Don's Dad and I a chance to go back to the hotel and have a much needed afternoon rest. By October 18th, 2005 all of Don's tubes had been removed, he had a blood transfusion, an albumin IV, and was up for his first walk. The doctor told us that the albumin was just to give the new liver a kick start.

Later on in the afternoon when we arrived at the ICU room, we found out that Don had been moved to a bed on the transplant unit. We headed there, my short legs walking in double time, so much so that I stepped in front of my husband and tripped over his feet, crashing to the hard floor. My knee was hurt, people came rushing. First one gentleman brought a chair, then another brought a wheelchair. I assured my husband that I was fine, and I knew that my knee was not broken. When my husband wheeled me into Donnie's room, Don was visibly upset and wondered what had happened. I was pushed around in the wheelchair for two days.

Much to our surprise and pleasure when we next visited Don, as we walked towards his room, he walked towards us using a walker. What a miracle once again – only six days and this determined man was out for a stroll, even though it was a slow stroll.

On October 20th, we stayed at the hotel until after lunch. When we arrived at the hospital Don's bed was empty. We checked with the nurse, and she told us that she had seen him go – that way – about half an hour earlier. Our first thought was that he might have gone to the cafeteria. Then we reasoned it would be too far, we were on the fifth floor and the elevators were way down the hall, and the cafeteria was on the main floor. He could not have gone there. We settled in the waiting room, watching both directions, and waiting for Don.

Waiting rooms are always interesting. You meet people who have even bigger challenges than you have, sharing stories gives strength and hope to others. I was beginning to get concerned about Don being out of his room so long, when I saw him coming slowly towards us with his walker. Yes, we couldn't believe it, he had been to the Subway fast food outlet on the main floor. There was a very satisfied look on his face. I am sure that he would have been rubbing his tummy if the stitches were not in the way.

When we were in Edmonton we were blessed to have many of our family members come to visit, and give us much needed and appreciated support. We had someone there every weekend, it was amazing. It was also amazing how a very private person like Don was anxious to show his incision to his family, even though he was not really able to see it himself. he was very proud of the way his body became the home of this precious new liver.

On October 21, Kathy and her twenty year old son arrived and checked into the same hotel as we were living in. Kathy had been there at the worst of times, and was surprised and thankful to see how well Don was doing and that his health was improving. Rob remarked about the complete turnaround he had noticed in Don from before the surgery to now. He was amazed. Every chance Don got he called his brother. They had often worked together, and these calls kept Don up to date with the latest news.

We were able to take Don out for awhile the next day. Every day we were in Edmonton, the weather was exceptionally good. Don enjoyed getting out, he was very sore, and needed help to get into our medium size truck. Don's Dad soon figured out that he just needed to drive close to the side walk and this worked well, with a gentle boost Don could get into the vehicle. We took Don out again the next day. We were beginning to get comfortable with this new lifestyle.

There was one thing that Don was disappointed about after the surgery, he and I were both surprised at the amount of fluid he was retaining. In all of our visits and preparation, this had never been explained, at least that we remembered. We asked about it and were told that it would go away and there was nothing to worry about. The organs all needed time to get well enough to do their work. Don did not expect to come out of surgery much bigger than when he went in. Now his abdominal cavity was full again and his legs were swollen, what he did not know was that there was swelling associated with the surgery that he had just undergone.

On October 24, 2005, Don was released from the hospital. We were thrilled to be taking him home to room 338 at the hotel. We would return to the hospital daily to check into the clinic to have blood work and therapy. This is the reason that you must be near the hospital for at least six weeks. Don's room at the hotel was very comfortable, he had his own television and bathroom. The door between our rooms was left ajar so I could check on him or go if he called. When you leave the hospital there are a number of medications to take at home, especially the anti-rejection medications. These medications called immune suppression drugs are meant to help protect your new liver from your own immune system.

You will have to take one or more of these drugs for the rest of your life, in addition to other medications. At first there will be antibiotics to help protect against infection, there are also medications to help protect your stomach from other medications. Your body may need some help, for a while to help get rid of water, or keeping up essential nutrients like potassium, magnesium, or iron. We had all of his medications lined up in his bathroom. The nurses had gone over the procedure carefully, emphasizing the importance of taking these medications every day and on a regular schedule.

On the morning of October 25, it seemed as if we were right back to life before the transplant. Don's breathing was becoming very difficult and he became extremely shaky. This severe shaking was something we had not seen before. We had an appointment at the liver clinic early the next day, where they did blood work, dressed his incision, took an x-ray, and he was to have a session of physiotherapy. All of these things occurred in different parts of the hospital, therefore we needed a wheelchair, to get to all of the places we needed to go. I was anxious to push my recovering Son in the wheelchair. I soon found out that this was not as easy as it looked. After bumping into a couple of walls I was relieved of my job by Don's Dad. Needless to say it is still not a good idea to mention the idea of me pushing a wheelchair to Don.

October 27 we were back at the liver clinic at the University Hospital at 8:00 A.M. where Don saw the liver specialist. This visit showed that Don's liver was functioning as it should be. They started an IV and administered two bottles of albumin, and Don was put on more diuretics, and they were trying to determine what was causing the shaking. After this appointment we returned to the hotel. He was physically uncomfortable, and the night was extremely hard, Don hollered, and called out, in nightmarish dreams. His legs were very swollen and painful, he slept fitfully, sleeping then waking, sleeping, then waking. It seemed just like before the surgery. It was at that time that Don became discouraged and disappointed.

On October 29, Don's aunt and uncle, as well as John and Sandra were arriving. They were pleased to hear that Don was out of the hospital, but when they saw him they were extremely concerned. After we arrived home, Don shared with me, that this period was the hardest of all. He wondered how he would make it through another day. Then I would cheerfully say – "Guess who is coming to see you?" With this he knew he had to muster enough strength to fight the fight another day, and so he carried on. Family and friends are such an important part of recovery.

Sunday morning (October 30) Don was very full of fluid, he was frightened – worried he was rejecting the liver. We wondered what could be happening. Monday morning I called the liver coordinator and said that we needed to get Don in, and was told that because Don had been discharged we had to go through emergency. Can you imagine what emergency in Edmonton University Hospital is like on a Monday morning? We checked in, Don's coordinator had told them that we were coming. They had his blood work, which showed that his body was not rejecting the liver. However Don was still troubled as to what could be happening to his body and this new gift which he had been given. We were there from 10:00 A.M. to 5:30 P.M.

along with a never ending room full of sick and not so sick people. Don stayed in the wheelchair, and became very anxious. The nurses checked his vital signs every hour, and gave us a blanket for him, and did everything they could to help us during that long day. I would get a snack for Don but he could not eat. That day might even have been harder than any other day we had. It was a terrible day. At 5:30 P.M. Don was taken into an emergency room where he spent the night. Once again Don was extremely ill, and we were again very concerned and frightened. The next morning he was moved to a room. The nurse that was caring for him that day was ready to leave on her shift change, she came to check him, then took her coat off and said, "I am not leaving here until something is done." She then proceeded to call the liver specialist, the internal medicine, and the lung specialists. Don received exceptional care at the U of A Hospital.

They were all there within ten minutes. After looking over reports, they quickly moved Don back to intensive care. They sedated Don for the night and all day Thursday. Another breathing tube was inserted. Many tests were done and the results were returned quickly. They found that Don had pneumonia. He was already on antibiotics, they increased the dose in hopes of getting this new infection under control. The test results showed that the shaking was being caused by one of the anti-rejection drugs. This crisis seemed to pass almost as fast as it had arrived. A draining tube was put in for a couple of days. This of course helped the breathing and the increased antibiotics worked on the pneumonia. He was kept in ICU until

November 6, when he was moved back into the liver transplant unit. He was kept on antibiotics until November 4th.

On November 11th, 2005, Don was up walking and pushing his IV along. On the 12th, he was doing well and looking good. We had experienced another critical week of his recovery. With the help of God and all of the wonderful doctors and nurses at the U of A Hospital we were back in a very comfortable space once again. The care at the U of A Hospital was exceptional, they were attentive in their care, and went to every possible length to help in the recovery process. One nurse remarked about Don's strong will to survive – she said – "You go into this very difficult situation, then you must be willing to fight for your life. It is not easy to do this, but is very necessary." Hope is a powerful part of any illness. On November 14, one month and one day since the surgery, Don was going to be released to go back to the hotel.

When the doctor came in that day, Don had a plan. He said, "With Dr. Meyer on the team, would it not be possible to go back to my own home, as we are only one hour from the Foothills Hospital? I have got to get my Mother home, she is seventy-one years old and fell the other day, and she really needs to be home."

I did not know about this plan. We were in for the long haul, and we did not want to go home one day sooner than it took for Don to be well enough to leave. On November 15th, the doctor released Don and turned him over to Dr. Meyer and the very capable care of the liver clinic in Calgary. Also his Mom was getting home. Don had therapy the morning of the 15th and I stood in the pharmacy being loaded up with medication and directions on each pill. The following medications became firmly entrenched in our minds:

- Cellcept – anti-rejection drug
- Septra – antibiotic
- Ranitidine – stomach acid control
- Docusate Sodium – to relieve constipation
- Acetamin – Pain relief
- ASA tablets – Blood thinner
- Sennosides – laxative
- Multi-vitamins
- Cloracillin – antibiotic
- Valgancyclovi – Antiviral
- Tacrolimus – Immune suppression / anti-rejection
- Ferrous Fumacite – Iron supplement
- Furosemide – a water pill to increase fluid output, and to keep blood pressure down.

All of these pills were well marked, but both Don and I needed to understand what they all were and when they needed to be taken. Don was supplied with a discharge teaching manual that walked one through a variety of potential scenarios that could happen after the transplant. He also had a discharge coordinator named Beth, who was at Dr. Meyer's office throughout the week to help with the recovery process. She willingly answered all of Don's questions, and sometimes I called her too. All of his appointments and care required following the transplant were done by Beth, another angel in our midst.

CHAPTER 11

The Birthday Present

November 15 was a special day in more ways than one as it was Don's 53rd birthday. We were loading our truck with the clothes and plastic containers we had arrived with only six weeks earlier. The weather was beautiful, and our Son was smiling from ear to ear anxious to be heading South, home to our small town. It was also Don's fifty-third birthday. On the way home Don leaned over and said to me "Mom this is the best birthday present I have ever had, or ever will have," as he patted his liver.

My reply was, "Yes, Don, yes."

After the long trip home Don went immediately down to the 'suite'. What a good place this was going to be for his recovery. His Dad and I were so happy, here we were with all of this behind us. We were ready for any little glitch that could come our way. There would be more trials in life, but we knew that we could face them. Don was blessed with his new liver, and he would treat it so very well.

The morning of November 16th, the day after we arrived home, Don came into the kitchen, fixed himself a bowl of cereal, took his pills, then put his jacket on. I questioned him as to where he was going. He planted a kiss on my cheek and said, "Mom I'm going out to live the rest of my life, in my own home."

"Well maybe this is too soon for me to let you go," I replied.

"Don't worry Mom, you'll be seeing a lot of me," Don replied.

With that I wiped a tear from my eye and said, "I am so proud of you Don. You have made me very happy. May God bless the rest of your life." The door gently closed behind him.

Later that day we had an appointment in Calgary to have blood tests done for Dr. Meyer's records, we were back again on the 18th for more tests, and our first appointment with Dr. Meyer was on November 29th. Dr. Meyer couldn't have been more pleased with the results of Don's surgery and with the way that his recovery was progressing. Don was still very sore, and had to move very carefully, due mainly to the large incision and the transplant procedure itself.

In the next few months Don had the start of one rejection and a couple of infections and a virus attack on his liver. Don was having blood work done twice a week, either in our home town or in the city. All of these infections and potential problems were caught early and treated quickly so they did not become major problems. Each time one of these problem arose we were reminded of the troubled times we had come through.

On December 15th, Don had an appointment with Dr. Thompson. This visit with her was even more special than our previous visits.

She held Don at arms length and said, "Look at you my Don! I am so proud of you! Look at your Mom how happy she is, her eyes are laughing. Stay here I am going to get Dr. Scott."

She rushed down the hall and came back with her wonderful husband. Saying "There is someone here I want you to see."

He stopped quickly inside the door and said, "I never thought I would see you again. I didn't think you would be able to fight this difficult battle." He reached his large hand out to shake Don's hand then said, "No, that is not good enough." He threw his arms around Don in a large hug and said, "God bless you, Don!"

After the moments of excitement were over, both doctors explained to Don how seldom it is that they ever have a patient that does exactly as they are told by their doctors. They do not have such complete results such as those which Don had just demonstrated to them. As the doctor wiped tears from his eyes, he shook Don's hand and left the room.

When Don was discharged from the hospital after his transplant he was given a book called the Discharge Teaching Manual, this outlined what would go on in the next few months. It explained what rejection is and how to recognize it, medications, infections, and follow up clinic visits, lab tests, and additional procedures which patients may or may not require. After a transplant your immune system is suppressed, so you must avoid contact with colds and flu as much as possible, you must also have a yearly flu shot. Don visited the liver clinic weekly for one month. Then twice a month, then soon only once a month. Then every three months.

On February 27, 2007, Dr. Meyer said, "Do you have anything to tell me?"

"No, not really," Don replied.

Dr. Meyer smiled and checked him over and said, "You have done a remarkable job in your recovery. I don't need to see you for six months. But, if you need me I am here."

Don has shared with me that saying you are going to quit drinking and actually accomplishing it takes more than a thought. It must come from within your heart and soul. You must feel it in your bones, your whole body must respond to your desire. Your eyes should portray the strength that you have to turn this thought into a reality. Don did just that.

Don continues to have blood work done on a regular basis.

During the first couple of months after Don got home, he began to remodel his house, being careful not to hurt himself. In the early spring he was back at Sandra's putting the finishing touches on her patio. Don reopened his own business and has built three homes for resale and is in the process of building another, all of this in the past ten months. His accomplishments have been remarkable. He looks great and keeps busy at constructive things. Thanks to his girlfriend they take drives to the hills and mountains, enjoy the scenery, and a good meal.

It took me about four months to learn to relax. It seemed as though much of the time I walked around my home waiting for something to happen, I never knew what, but surely something. After adjusting I got busy with my church work and refilled my schedule with regular things. This man, my Son, that only fifteenth months ago made the decision to change his life is living proof that it can be done.

In Don's case he could not have survived without a liver transplant. Too many times he was near death, with the help of God, the doctors, and the donor he was able to be saved. Christmas of 2005, my gift from Don was a beautiful silver plate, engraved with a cross, and the words; "Thanks for your prayers and strength ~ Love Don." In the gift box there was also a little porcelain guardian angel, once again my Son touched my heart.

The third Sunday we were home Don came by the house as we were ready to go to church. I was surprised because he knew we would be leaving at that time.

"Mom, I think I will go to church with you – just this time. I want the Man Upstairs to know that I am thankful to Him, also all of your friends at church who prayed for me."

How proud his Dad and I were to be sitting beside this changed man. Yes, our prayers were answered.

To God be the Glory for the things He had done. With the help of God we saved our Son.

Epilogue

I AM SURE by now, that it is evident, that there would not have been a story to tell without a donor. My Son would not have lived the one and a half years that the doctor predicted. Never give up if you have someone who needs help. Reach out for help if you are in need. There are so many people who are willing to be there for you. The gift of life is one way you can help others. Organ and tissue transplantation, is a modern medical miracle through which thousands of lives are saved or enhanced each year. For organ and tissue donors and their families, it is a chance to give life, a chance to help others at a time when it may seem that so much has been taken away. For recipients like my Son it is life. Anyone, regardless of age or race, can donate organs and tissues. The age and the health of a donor are not as important as the condition of their organs and tissues. If you decide to be an organ donor, you might wonder if there would be a conflict in saving your life and donating your organs and tissues, you can be assured that everything that can be done to save your life will be.

The doctors looking after the donor cannot be a member of the recipient's transplant team, or be associated with the proposed recipient in any way. Organs and tissues are very carefully removed, and incisions are closed with the same care provided to living people. Even with a signed donor card, organ and tissue donation cannot proceed without the consent of the family – make them aware of your wishes.

There are many causes of liver disease, alcohol being only one of them. Alcoholism is a national epidemic, it is the third leading cause of preventable death. There is free treatment and centres everywhere. There are people who have been there, done that, and are ready to help others. Never give up on someone you love, or a family member. You may not always succeed – but what if you would have – can you take that chance. I couldn't.

I heard a saying on television the other day – Beware it (alcoholism) is everywhere, and so it is, you are not alone with this disease. Combating the life revolving around alcohol requires your greatest efforts, it also brings the greatest reward you have ever known. Life will take on a whole new meaning. You can come to feel in ways you have never known before. You can become beautiful, and best of all you will be free.

It's In The Valleys That I Grow
by Jane Eggleston

Sometimes life seems hard to bear,
Full of sorrow, trouble and woe
It's then I have to remember
That it's in the valley's that I grow

If I always stayed on the mountaintop
And never experienced pain,
I would never appreciate God's love
And would be living in vain.

I have so much to learn
And my growth is very slow,
Sometimes I need the mountain tops,
But it's in the valleys I grow.

I do not always understand
Why things happen as they do,
But I am very sure of one thing.
My Lord will see me through.

*My little valleys are nothing
When I picture Christ on the cross
He went through the valley of Death;
His victory was Satan's loss.*

*Forgive me Lord, for complaining
When I'm feeling so very low.
Just give me a gentle reminder
That it's in the valleys I grow.*

*Continue to strengthen me, Lord
And use my life each day
To share your love with others
And help them find their way.*

*Thank you for valleys, Lord
For this one thing I know
The mountain tops are glorious
But it's in the valley's I grow!*

Acknowledgments

To the Foothills Hospital for their special care and concern for our son, It was your ongoing support that kept Don alive so he could receive the transplant that gave him new life. We will be forever grateful

To the University of Alberta Hospital for their excellent care and treatment during the transplant process.

I am grateful to Julaine for her willingness to type all of the drafts and for her helpful suggestions. The time we spent together is a memorable part of this story.

Thanks to Barb for her encouragement and editing. How fortunate I am to have met you.

To Nina for her beautiful artwork

To Prairie Home Design for the back cover image.

To my children for their willingness to listen when I needed to talk, which was often. Thank you for your support in this endeavor.

To my grandson Rob for telling me –
"The writing is awesome."

To my husband Don for his encouragement, and strength as we journeyed together.

To my son for your strength, courage, and willingness to share.

Resources Referenced In The Creation of This Book

Liver Transplant Pre-op Teaching Manual
- *Supplied by Southern Alberta Transplant Clinic.*

Liver Transplant Program
- *University of Alberta Hospital*

Canadian Liver Foundation
- *National Office, Toronto, Ontario, Canada*

Discharge Teaching Manual
- *University of Alberta Hospital*

ISBN 142512845-9